Wom...

A Short H...   ...a Great
Movement

Millicent Garrett Fawcett
President of the National Union of
Women's Suffrage Societies

It is not to be thought of that the flood
Of British freedom, which to the open sea
Of the world's praise, from dark antiquity
Hath flowed "with pomp of waters unwithstood" —
Road by which all might come and go that would,
And bear out freights of worth to foreign lands;
That this most famous stream in bogs and sands
Should perish, and to evil and to good
Be lost for ever. In our halls is hung
Armoury of the invincible knights of old:
We must be free or die, who speak the tongue
That Shakespeare spake — *the faith and morals hold*
Which Milton held. In everything we're sprung
Of earth's first blood, have titles manifold.
- W. Wordsworth.

Table of Contents

CHAPTER I
THE BEGINNINGS

We suffragists have no cause to be ashamed of the founders of our movement —

"In everything we're sprung
Of earth's first blood, have titles manifold."

Mary Wollstonecraft[1] started the demand of women for political liberty in England, Condorcet in France,[2] and the heroic group of anti-slavery agitators in the United States. It is true that Horace Walpole called Mary Wollstonecraft "a hyena in petticoats." But this proves nothing except his profound ignorance of her character and aims. Have we not in our own time heard the ladies who first joined the Primrose League described by an excited politician as "filthy witches"? The epithet of course was as totally removed from any relation to the facts as that which Horace Walpole applied to Mary Wollstonecraft. William Godwin's touching memoir of his wife, Mr. Kegan Paul's

---

[1] *Vindication of the Rights of Women*, published in 1792.

[2] See Le vote des Femmes, pp. 16-22, par Ferdinand Buisson, Député de la Seine et Président de la Commission du Suffrage Universelle. Condorcet had a predecessor in Mademoiselle Jars de Gournay, the friend of Montaigne. See Miss E. Sichel's Michel de Montaigne, p. 137.

William Godwin: his Friends and Contemporaries, and Mrs. Pennell's Biography show Mary Wollstonecraft as a woman of exceptionally pure and exalted character. Her sharp wits had been sharpened by every sort of personal misfortune; they enabled her to pierce through all shams and pretences, but they never caused her to lower her high sense of duty; they never embittered her or caused her to waver in her allegiance to the pieties of domestic life. Her husband wrote of her soon after her death, "She was a worshipper of domestic life." If there is anything in appearance, her face in the picture in the National Portrait Gallery speaks for her. Southey wrote of her, that of all the lions of the day whom he had seen "her face was the best, infinitely the best."

The torch which was lighted by Mary Wollstonecraft was never afterwards extinguished; there are glimpses of its light in the poems of her son-in-law Shelley. The frequent references to the principle of equality between men and women in the "Revolt of Islam" will occur to every reader.

In 1810 Sydney Smith, in the *Edinburgh Review*, wrote one of the most brilliant and witty articles which even he ever penned in defence of an extension of the means of a sound education to women.

In 1813 Mrs. Elizabeth Fry began to visit prisoners in Newgate, and shocked those who, citing the parrot cry "woman's place is home," thought a good woman had no duties outside its walls. She had children of her own, but this did not shut her heart to the wretched waifs for whom she founded a school in prison. A little after this England began to be stirred by the agitation which resulted in the passing of the Reform Bill of 1832. It is one of life's little ironies that James Mill, the founder of the Philosophical Radicals, and the father of John Stuart Mill, who laid the foundation of the modern suffrage movement, was among those who, in the early nineteenth century, justified the exclusion of women from all political rights. In an Essay on "Government" published in 1823 as an appendix to the fifth edition of the *Encyclopaedia Britannica*, he dismissed in a sentence all claim of women to share in the benefits and protection of representative government, stating that their interests were sufficiently protected by the enfranchisement of their husbands and fathers. It is true that this did not pass unchallenged; a book in reply was published (1825) by William Thomson. This book had a preface by Mrs. Wheeler, at whose instigation it was written.[3]

The Reform Movement was agitating the whole country at this period, and political excitement led to political riots, burning of buildings, and general orgies of massacre and destruction. The Government of the day had their share in the blunders and stupidities which led to these crimes, and

---

[3] Helen Blackburn's *Record of Women's Suffrage*, also *Women in English Life*, by Miss Georgina Hill. Mrs. Wheeler's daughter Rosina, married Mr. Lytton Bulwer, afterwards the first Lord Lytton. The present Earl of Lytton is thus the great-grandson of the lady who prompted the reply to James Mill's article referred to in the text.

in none were these qualities more conspicuous than in the riot at Manchester, which came to be known as the Peterloo Massacre in August 1819, in which six people were killed and about thirty seriously injured.

What connects it with the subject of these pages has already been hinted at. Women as well as men had been ridden down by the cavalry; they were present at the meeting not merely as spectators, but as taking an active part in the Reform Movement. A picture of the Peterloo Massacre, now in the Manchester Reform Club, is dedicated to "Henry Hunt, Esq., the chairman of the meeting and *to the Female Reformers of Manchester* and the adjacent towns who were exposed to and suffered from the wanton and furious attack made on them by that brutal armed force, the Manchester and Cheshire Yeomanry Cavalry." The picture represents women in every part of the fray, and certainly taking their share in its horrors. In the many descriptions of the event, no word of reprobation has come to my notice of the women who were taking part in the meeting; they were neither "hyenas" nor "witches," but patriotic women helping their husbands and brothers to obtain political liberty; in a word, they were working for men and not for themselves, and this made an immense difference in the judgment meted out to them. However, it is quite clear that even as long ago as 1819 the notion that women have nothing to do with politics was in practice rejected by the political common-sense of Englishmen. No one doubted that women were, and ought to be, deeply interested in what concerned the political well-being of their country.

Some political antiquarians in this country have expressed their conviction that in early times when the institution of feudalism was the strongest political force in England, women exercised electoral rights in those cases where they were entitled as landowners or as freewomen of certain towns to do so.[4] This view has been combated by other authorities, and has not been accepted in the law courts, where special emphasis has been laid on the fact that no authentic case of a woman having actually cast a vote, as of right, in a Parliamentary election can be produced. The claim that in ancient times women did exercise the franchise, whether capable of being established or not, certainly does not deserve to be dismissed as in itself absurd and incredible. I believe it has been called by some anti-suffragists "an impudent imposture," in the most approved style of the "what-I-know-not-is-not-knowledge" pedant. Whatever it may be, it is not this. In a book published in 1911,[5] there is a passage which goes far to prove that even as late as 1807 the right of women possessing the necessary legal

---

[4] This view has also been supported in France, see *Le vote des Femmes*, by Ferdinand Buisson, for evidence of women having in ancient times voted and sat in the Parlements of France. Taine also mentions the Countess of Perigord sitting in the Ftate of her province prior to the Revolution *(Les Origines de la France Contemporaine*, par H. Taine, vol. i. p. 104).

[5] *Annals of a Yorkshire House*, vol. ii. p. 319.

qualification to vote in Parliamentary elections was recognised as being in existence. One of the Spencer Stanhopes was a candidate during the general election of 1807, and Mrs. Spencer Stanhope writes to her son, John, that her husband's party was so certain of success that they had announced that their women folk need not vote. "Your father was at Wakefield canvassing yesterday... They determined not to admit the ladies to vote, which is extraordinary and very hard, considering how few privileges we poor females have. Should it come to a very close struggle, I daresay they will then call upon the ladies, and in that case every self-respecting woman should most certainly refuse her assistance."

The contention is that the Reform Act of 1832, by substituting the words "male person" in lieu of the word "man" in the earlier Acts, first placed upon the women of this country the burden of a statutory disability. This process, it is argued, was repeated in the Municipal Corporation Act of 1835, and is the reason why the admission of women to the municipal franchise in 1870 is spoken of in many of our suffrage publications as the "*Restoration*" of the municipal suffrage to women. The point appears more of antiquarian than of practical interest. If substantiated, it only illustrates anew the fact that under feudalism, and as long as feudalism survived, property rather than human beings had a special claim to representation, but it assumed a larger degree of importance from what followed in 1850 and 1868.

In 1850 Lord Brougham's Act was passed, which enacted that in all Acts of Parliament "words importing the masculine gender shall be deemed to include females unless the contrary is expressly provided." In the Reform Bill of 1867 the words "male person" were abandoned, and the word "man" was substituted, and many lawyers and others believed that under Lord Brougham's Act of 1850 women were thereby enfranchised. Under this belief, the reasons for which were set forth by Mr. Chisholm Anstey, barrister and ex-M.P., in two legal pamphlets published, one just before and one just after the passing of the Reform Bill of 1867, a large number of women rate-payers claimed before the revising barristers in 1868 to be placed upon the Parliamentary register. Under the able leadership of Miss Lydia Becker 5346 women householders of Manchester made this claim, 1341 in Salford, 857 in Broughton and Pendleton, 1 lady in S.E. Lancashire, a county constituency, 239 in Edinburgh, and a few in other parts of Scotland. The revising barristers in most of these cases declined to place the women's names on the register; and in order to get a legal decision, four cases were selected and argued before the Court of Common Pleas on November 7, 1868. The judges were the Lord Chief Justice Bovill, with the Justices Willes, Keating, and Byles. Sir John (afterwards Lord) Coleridge, and Dr. Pankhurst were counsel for the appellants. The case (technically known as Chorlton v. Lings) was given against the women, on the express ground that although

13

the word "man" in an Act of Parliament must be held to include women, "*this did not apply to the privileges granted by the State.*" This judgment, therefore, established as law that "the same words in the same Act of Parliament shall for the purpose of voting apply to men only, but for the purpose of taxation shall include women."[6]

Some women's names had been accepted by revising barristers, and were already upon the register. A question was raised whether they could remain there. The barrister in charge of this case, Mr. A. Russell, Q.C., argued that when once the names were upon the register, if they had not been objected to they must remain; one of the judges thereupon remarked that if this were so there would be no power to remove the name of *a dog or a horse* from the register if once it had been inscribed upon it. This was eloquent of the political status of women, identifying it by implication with that of the domestic animals. *The Times*, in anticipation of the Chorlton *v.* Lings case coming on for hearing, had an article on November 3, 1868, in which it said: "If one supposes it ever was the intention of the legislature to give women a vote, and if they do get it, it will be by a sort of accident, in itself objectionable, though, in its practical consequences, perhaps harmless enough. On the other hand, if they are refused, *the nation*

---

[6] Report of the Manchester National Society for Women's Suffrage, 1869.

will, no doubt, be formally and in the light of day committing itself through its judicial tribunal, to the dangerous doctrine that representation need not go along with taxation." With the decision in Chorlton *v.* Lings, the last chance of women getting the suffrage by "a sort of accident" vanishes, and very few of us can now regret it, for the long struggle to obtain suffrage has been a great education for women, not only politically, but also in courage, perseverance, endurance, and comradeship with each other.

If the nineteenth century was a time of education for women, it was no less a time of education for men. We have not yet arrived at an equal moral standard for men and women, but we have travelled a long way on the road leading to it. A George I. openly surrounding himself with mistresses, and shutting up his wife for life in a fortress for levity of behaviour; a George IV. who measured with similar inequality his own and his wife's connubial transgressions, would not be tolerated in the England of the twentieth century. The awakening of women to a sense of their wrongs before the law was a leading feature of the women's movement in the early nineteenth century. The Hon. Mrs. Norton, the beautiful and gifted daughter of Tom Sheridan, a reigning toast, a society beauty, and with literary accomplishments sufficient to secure her an independent income from her pen, was subjected to every sort of humiliation and anguish as a wife and mother which the mean and cruel nature of her husband could devise. Mr. Norton brought an action against Lord Melbourne for the seduction of his wife, and the jury decided without leaving the box that Lord Melbourne was wholly innocent. This did not prevent the petty malice of her husband from depriving Mrs. Norton entirely of her three infant children, one of whom died from an accident which ought never to have happened if the child had been duly cared for. To read her life[7] is comparable to being present at a vivisection. Mrs. Norton had one weapon. She could make herself heard; she wrote a pamphlet in 1836 called "*The Natural Claim of a Mother to the Custody of her Children as affected by the Common Law Right of the Father.*" One result which followed from Mrs. Norton's sufferings, coupled with her power of giving public expression to them, was the passing of Serjeant Talfourd's Act in 1839, called the Infants' Custody Act, giving a mother the right of access to her children until they are seven years old. This is the first inroad on the monopoly on the part of the father of absolute control over his children created by the English law. The division of legal rights over their children between fathers and mothers has been described by a lawyer as extremely simple — the fathers have all and the mothers none. Serjeant Talfourd's Act did not do much to redress this gross injustice; but it did something, and marks the beginning of a new epoch.

---

[7] *The Life of Mrs. Norton*, by Miss Jane Gray Perkins (John Murray).

Little by little things began to change. Mrs. Somerville and Miss Caroline Herschell were elected members of the Royal Astronomical Society in 1835. Mrs. Browning wrote "Aurora Leigh," and thereby touched the whole woman's question with an artist's hand. Thackeray, in *Esmond*, pointed the finger of scorn at the "politicians and coffee-house wiseacres," who are full of oratorical indignation against the tyrannies of the Emperor or the French King, and wonders how they, who are tyrants too in their way, govern their own little dominions at home, where each man reigns absolute. "When the annals of each little reign are shown to the Supreme Master, under whom we hold sovereignty, histories will be laid bare of household tyrants as cruel as Amurath, and as savage as Nero, and as reckless and dissolute as Charles." This was a new note in literature. Mrs. Jameson and the Brontë sisters contributed much in the same key. Anne Knight, a Quaker lady of Quiet House, Chelmsford, issued about 1847 a small leaflet boldly claiming a share for women in political freedom. There can be little doubt that the presence of a pure and virtuous young woman upon the throne had its influence in leading people to question seriously whether there was any real advantage to the nation at large in shutting out from direct political power all women who were not queens. In 1848[8] Mr. Disraeli, in the House of

---

[8] The date of this speech is given in Miss Blackburn's *Record of Woman's Suffrage* as 1866, the only mistake I have found in her careful and faithful history.

Commons, had said, "In a country governed by a woman — where you allow women to form part of the other estate of the realm — peeresses in their own right, for example — where you allow women not only to hold land but to be ladies of the manor and hold legal courts — where a woman by law may be a churchwarden and overseer of the poor — I do not see, where she has so much to do with the State and Church, on what reasons, if you come to right, she has not a right to vote."

Other influences were operating to open political activity to women. Their help and co-operation were warmly welcomed by the Anti-Corn Law League. Cobden, at one of the great meetings of the League held in Covent Garden Theatre in 1845, said that he wished women could vote. A few years later than this the Sheffield Female Political Association passed a resolution in favour of women's suffrage, and presented a petition in this sense to the House of Lords. The refusal to allow women who had been duly appointed as delegates in the United States to take their places in the Anti-Slavery Congress held in London in 1840 roused a great deal of controversy, especially as William Lloyd Garrison, the leader of the Anti-Slavery Movement in America,[9] declared that if the ladies were excluded he would share their exclusion with them; he did this, and sat with them in a side gallery,

---

[9] See the interesting picture in the staircase of the National Portrait Gallery, London.

taking no part in the discussion. The opponents of the women took refuge, as they have so often done before and since, in an affirmation that they were the special repositories of the Divine Will on the subject, and declared that it was contrary to the ordinances of the Almighty that women should take part in the Congress. The treatment they had received in London naturally caused great indignation on the part of the American ladies, among whom were Elizabeth Cady Stanton and Lucretia Mott. When they returned to their own country they immediately began to work for the political enfranchisement of women, and the first Women's Rights Convention was held in the United States at Seneca Falls in 1848. This was the beginning of definite work for women's suffrage in the United States.

In England in the 'fifties came the Crimean War, with the deep stirring of national feeling which accompanied it, and the passion of gratitude and admiration which was poured forth on Miss Florence Nightingale for her work on behalf of our wounded soldiers. It was universally felt that there was work for women, even in war — the work of cleansing, setting in order, breaking down red tape, and soothing the vast sum of human suffering which every war is bound to cause. Miss Nightingale's work in war was work that never had been done until women came forward to do it, and her message to her countrywomen was educate yourselves, prepare, make ready; never imagine that your task can be done by instinct, without training and preparation. Painstaking study, she insisted, was just as necessary as a preparation for women's work as for men's work; and she bestowed the whole of the monetary gift offered her by the gratitude of the nation to form training-schools for nurses at St. Thomas's and King's College Hospitals.

When a fire is once kindled many things will serve as fuel which to a superficial glance would seem to have no connection with it. The sufferings and torture of women during the Indian Mutiny heroically borne helped people to see that Empire is built on the lives of women as well as on the lives of men.

"*On the bones of the English/ The English flag is stayed,*" means that women as well as men have laid down their lives for their country.

In 1857 the movement among women for political recognition was stimulated in quite a different way. In that year the Divorce Act was passed, and, as is well known, set up by law a different moral standard for men and women. Under this Act, which is still in force (1911), a man can obtain the dissolution of his marriage if he can prove one act of infidelity on the part of his wife; but a woman cannot get her marriage dissolved unless she can prove that her husband has been guilty both of infidelity and cruelty. Mr. Gladstone vehemently opposed this Bill. It is said that "in a ten hours' debate on a single clause he made no less than twenty-nine speeches, some of them of considerable length."[10] All these things prepared the way for the movement which took definite shape in the next decade.

---

[10] Morley's *Life of Gladstone*, vol. i. p. 571.

CHAPTER II
WOMEN'S SUFFRAGE QUESTION IN PARLIAMENT — FIRST STAGE

"All who live in a country should take an interest in that country, love that country, and the vote gives that sense of interest, fosters that love."

— Rt. Hon. W. E. Gladstone.

The women's suffrage question in 1860 was on the point of entering a new phase — the phase of practical politics. Parliamentary Reform was again before the country; the principles of representation were constantly discussed in newspapers, and in every social circle where intelligent men and women met.

James Mill's article on "Government," referred to in Chapter I., has been described as being "out of sight the most important in the series of events which culminated in the passing of the Reform Act of 1832."[11] The works of his son, John Stuart Mill, had a similar influence on the series of events which led up to the passing of the Reform Act of

---

[11] *James Mill: a Biography*, by Alexander Bain, LL.D., p. 215.

1867. But whereas James Mill had specifically excluded women from his argument, John Mill as specifically and with great force and vigour included them.

In his *Political Economy*, and in his collected essays, and, of course, in his *Liberty*, it was easy to perceive that he strongly condemned the condition of subordination to which the mass of women had been from time immemorial condemned. But in his *Representative Government*, published in 1861, he put forward in a few eloquent pages of powerful argument the case for the extension of the suffrage to women, showing that all the arguments by which the principles of representative government were supported were equally applicable to woman.[12]

The volumes of his correspondence, published in 1908, show how constantly his mind dwelt on the grave injustice to women involved by their exclusion from political rights, and also how deeply he was convinced that the whole of society loses by treating them as if they had no responsibility for the right conduct of national affairs. It was an enormous advantage to the whole women's movement, not only in England, but all over the world, that it had for its leader and champion a man in the front rank of political philosophers and thinkers. He formed a school at the universities, and in all centres of intellectual activity, and from that school a large number of the chief

---

[12] *Representative Government*, by J. S. Mill, pp. 175-180.

leaders and supporters of the women's movement have been derived.

As early as 1851 an essay on the "Enfranchisement of Women" had appeared in the *Westminster Review*. It had been written by Mrs. J. S. Mill, and took the form of a review of the proceedings of a Convention of Women held in Worcester, Massachusetts, in the previous year to promote the cause of the political enfranchisement of women.

The essay is a complete and masterly statement of the case for the emancipation of women. The terminology is a little out of date, but the state of mind which she exposes is perennial. We can all, for instance, recognise the applicability of the following sentences to the present time: —

"For with what truth or rationality could the suffrage be termed universal while half the human species remain excluded from it? To declare that a voice in the government is the right of all, and demand it only for a part — the part, namely, to which the claimant belongs — is to renounce even the appearance of principle. The Chartist, who denies the suffrage to women, is a Chartist only because he is not a lord; he is one of those levellers who would level only down to themselves."[13]

This essay, with its clear, pointed, and epigrammatic style, produced a great effect on the more cultivated

---

[13] *Dissertations and Discussions*, by J. S. Mill, vol. ii. p. 417.

section of public opinion. If Mrs. Mill had lived longer she would probably have inaugurated the practical organisation of a women's enfranchisement movement, but she died in the autumn of 1858. What her death meant to her husband he has left on record in glowing and touching words, and in his loneliness he endeavoured "because she would have wished it," to make the best of what life was left to him, "to work on for her purposes with such diminished strength as could be derived from thoughts of her and communion with her memory."[14]

Shortly before the general election of 1865 Mr. Mill was invited by a considerable body of electors of the Borough of Westminster to offer himself as a candidate. In reply he made the plainest possible statement of his political views, including his conviction that women were entitled to representation in Parliament. It was the first time that women's suffrage had ever been brought before English electors, and the fact that after having announced himself as strongly in favour of it Mr. Mill was elected, gave a place to women's suffrage in practical politics.

The situation in Parliament, as regards Parliamentary Reform, at the time of Mr. Mill's election was very like what it is now in respect of women's suffrage. Parliament had been playing with the subject for a great many years. Reform Bills had been introduced, voted for, and abandoned again and again. The real reformers were

---

[14] *Autobiography*, p. 241

growing impatient. I, myself, heard John Bright say about this time or a little later that he began to think the best way of carrying a Reform Bill was to tell working men that "a good rifle could be bought for £2." Candidates who stood for election pledged themselves to Parliamentary Reform, but year after year went by and nothing was done. Each party brought forward Reform Bills, but neither party really wished to enfranchise the working classes. Before 1867 the total electorate only numbered a little over one million voters. The Reform Bill of 1867 more than doubled this number. It is not in human nature for members of Parliament really to like a very large increase in the number of their constituents. Besides the extra trouble and expense involved, there was in 1865 another deterrent — terror. Those who held power feared the working classes. Working men were supposed to be the enemies of property, and working men were in an enormous numerical majority over all other classes combined. "You must not have the vote because there are so many of you" was a much more effective argument when used against working men than it is when used against women; because the working classes are fifteen or sixteen times more numerous than all other classes combined, whereas women are only slightly in excess of men.[15] On one excuse or another the Reform Bills

---

[15] The census of 1911 shows that the excess of women over men is in the proportion of 1068 women to 1000 men, and that this proportion has changed but little during the last hundred and ten years.

constantly brought before Parliament were dropped or burked in one of the thousand ways open to the experienced Parliamentarian for getting rid of measures which he has to appear to support, but to which he is in reality opposed. The time had come, however, after 1865, when it became apparent that the game was up, and that a Reform Bill would have to be passed. It was to this Parliament that Mill was elected, and in which in 1867, as an amendment to the Reform Bill, he raised the question of the enfranchisement of women. His motion was to omit the word "man" and insert the word "person" in the enfranchising clause. Of this he says himself that it was by far the most important public service that he was able to perform as a member of Parliament. Seventy-three members voted with him and 196 against him; with the addition of pairs and tellers the total number supporting women's suffrage was over 80. This amount of support surpassed all expectations. Before the debate and division it was uncertain whether women's suffrage would command more than a few stray votes in the House. Mr. Mill's masterly speech, grave and high-toned, made a deep impression. Perhaps the thing that pleased him most was the fact that John Bright voted with him. He was known to be an opponent of women's suffrage, but he was fairly won over by the force of Mill's speech. Those who watched him sitting in the corner seat of the front row on the left-hand side of the Speaker, just below Mr. Mill, saw his whole expression and demeanour change as the speech proceeded. His defiant, mocking expression changed to one that was serious and thoughtful; no one but Mill ever had the moral and mental strength to wrestle with him again successfully. It was the first and last time he ever gave a vote for women's suffrage.

It is an oft-told tale how in the previous year a little committee of workers had been formed to promote a Parliamentary petition from women in favour of women's suffrage. It met in the house of Miss Garrett, (now Mrs. Garrett Anderson, M.D.), and included Mrs. Bodichon, Miss Emily Davies, Mrs. Peter Taylor, Miss Rosamond Davenport Hill, and other well-known women. They consulted Mr. Mill about the petition, and he promised to present it if they could collect as many as a hundred names. After a fortnight's work they secured 1499, including many of the most distinguished women of the day, such as Mrs. Somerville, Frances Power Cobbe, Florence Nightingale, Harriet Martineau, Miss Swanwick, Mrs. Josephine Butler, Lady Anna Gore Langton, Mrs. William Grey. In June 1866 Miss Garrett and Miss Emily Davies took the petition down to the House, entering by way of Westminster Hall. They were a little embarrassed by the size of the roll in their charge, and deposited it with the old apple-woman, who hid it under her stall. The ladies did not know how to find Mr. Mill, when at that moment Mr. Fawcett passed through Westminster Hall and at once offered to go in search of him. Mr. Mill was much amused on his arrival when he found the petition was hidden away under the apple-woman's stall; but he was greatly delighted by the large number of names which had been obtained, and exclaimed, "Ah, this I can brandish with great effect."[16]

It was in 1867 that the Reform Bill was carried, and Mr. Mill's Women's Suffrage Amendment defeated on May 20th. The testing of the actual legal effect of the passing of the Bill upon the political status of women (already described in Chapter I.) took place in 1868. These events caused a great deal of thought and discussion with regard to women's position in relation to the State and public duties in general; and it is as certain as anything which is insusceptible of absolute proof can be, that to the interest excited by the claim of women to the Parliamentary vote was due the granting to them of the Municipal Franchise in 1869; and also that in 1870, when the first great Education Act was passed, they were not only given the right to vote for members of School Boards, but also the right to be elected upon them. At the first School Board election, which took place in London in November 1870, Miss Elizabeth Garrett, M.D., and Miss Emily Davies were returned as members. Miss Garrett was at the head of the poll in her constituency — Marylebone. She polled more than 47,000 votes, the largest number, it was said at the time, which had ever been bestowed upon any candidate in any election in England. In Manchester Miss Becker was

---

[16] *Record of Women's Suffrage*, by Helen Blackburn, pp. 53, 54, 55.

elected a member of the first School Board, and was continuously re-elected for twenty years, until her death in 1890. In Edinburgh Miss Flora Stevenson was elected to the first School Board, and was continuously re-elected for thirty-three years until her death in 1905. From the date of her election she was appointed by her colleagues to act as convener of some of their most important committees, and in 1900 was unanimously elected the chairman of the board; she retained this most honourable and responsible post until the end of her life.

The connection between the election of the ladies just mentioned — and other instances might be added — with the suffrage movement is strongly indicated by the fact that they were, without exception, the leading personal representatives of the suffrage movement in the various places in which they respectively lived. Miss Garrett and Miss Davies, as just described, helped to organise the suffrage petition, which they handed to Mr. Mill in 1866; Miss Becker was the head and front of the suffrage movement in Manchester, and Miss Flora Stevenson in Edinburgh. These ladies had taken an active part in starting the women's suffrage societies in their own towns. Five important societies came into existence almost simultaneously in London, Manchester, Edinburgh, Bristol, and Birmingham, and as they almost immediately devised a plan for combining individual responsibility with united action, they formed the nucleus of the National Union of Women's Suffrage Societies, which has become the largest organisation of the kind in the United Kingdom, and in October 1911 numbered 305 societies, a number which is constantly and rapidly increasing.

With the suffrage work carried on by the societies, other work for improving the legal status of women, resisting encroachments upon their constitutional liberties, and improving their means of education went on with vigour, sobriety, and enthusiasm; these qualities were combined in a remarkable degree, and were beyond all praise. It has been remarked that the successful conduct of every great change needs the combination of the spirit of order with the spirit of audacity. It was the good fortune of the women's movement in England to secure both these. The suffrage societies from the first saw the necessity of keeping to suffrage work only; but the same individuals in a different capacity were labouring with heroic persistence and untiring zeal to lift up the conditions of women's lives in other ways; thus to Mrs. Jacob Bright, Mrs. Wolstenholme Elmy, Mrs. Duncan M'Laren, and Mrs. Pochin, we owe the first Married Women's Property Act, and also the Guardianship of Children Act; to Mrs. Bodichon and Miss Davies, Henry Sidgwick and Russell Gurney, the opening of university education to women; to Miss Garrett (now Mrs. Anderson), Dr. Elizabeth Blackwell, and Miss Jex Blake, the opening of the medical profession; to Mrs. Josephine Butler, and Mr. and Mrs. Sheldon Amos, Sir James Stanfeld, and Mr. James Stuart, the repeal of the Contagious Diseases Acts (passed in 1866 and 1868); to Mrs. William Grey, Miss Sherriff and Miss Gurney, the creation of good secondary schools for girls. I am well aware that in this bald recital I have omitted the names of many noble, conscientious, and self-sacrificing workers for the great causes to which they had devoted themselves; I cannot even attempt to make my list exhaustive; I have but selected from a very large number, all ardent suffragists, a few names that stand out pre-eminently in my memory among the glorious company whose efforts laid the foundations on which we at the present day are still building the superstructure of equal opportunity and equal justice for women and men.

As an illustration of how the tone has changed in regard to the personal and proprietary rights of women I can give a little story which fell within my own experience. In the 'seventies I was staying with my father at a time when he had convened in his house a meeting of Liberal electors of East Suffolk. We were working then for a Married Women's Property Bill. The first Act passed in 1870 gave a married woman the right to possess her *earnings*, but not any other property. I had petition forms with me, and thought the "Liberal" meeting would afford me a good opportunity of getting signatures to it. So I took it round and explained its aim to the quite average specimens of the Liberal British farmer. "Am I to understand you, ma'am, that if this Bill passes, and my wife have a matter of a hundred pound left to her, I should have to *ask* her for it?" said one of them. The idea appeared monstrous that a man could not take his wife's £100 without even going through the form of asking her for it.

But we were making way steadily. It is true that Mr. Mill was not re-elected in 1868, but Mr. Jacob Bright succeeded him as the leader in the House of Commons of the women's suffrage movement. The second reading of his, the first Women's Suffrage Bill, was carried on May 4, 1870, by 124 to 91. Further progress was, however, prevented, mainly in consequence of the opposition of the Government, and on the motion to go into committee on May 12, the Bill was defeated by 220 to 94.

From the beginning women's suffrage had never been a party question. In the first division, that on Mr. Mill's Amendment to the Reform Bill, the 73 members who voted for women's suffrage included about 10 Conservatives, and one of them, the Rt. Hon. Russell Gurney, Q.C., Recorder of London, was one of the tellers in the division. The great bulk of the supporters of the principle of women's suffrage were then and still are Liberals and Radicals, but from the outset we have always had an influential group of Conservative supporters. And it is indicative of the general growth of the movement that among the large majority secured for the second reading of Sir George Kemp's Bill in May 5, 1911, 79 were Conservatives, a number in excess of the total of those who supported Mr. Mill's amendment in 1867. Sir Stafford Northcote (afterwards Lord Iddesleigh) was among the friends of women's suffrage, and so was Sir

Algernon Borthwick (afterwards Lord Glenesk), the proprietor and editor of *The Morning Post*. Support from the Conservative side of the house was greatly encouraged in 1873 by a letter written by Mr. Disraeli in reply to a memorial signed by over 11,000 women. The memorial had been forwarded by Mr. William Gore Langton, M.P., and was thus acknowledged: —

"Dear Gore Langton, — I was much honoured by receiving from your hands the memorial signed by 11,000 women of England — among them some illustrious names — thanking me for my services in attempting to abolish the anomaly that the Parliamentary franchise attached to a household or property qualification, when possessed by a woman, should not be exercised, though in all matters of local government when similarly qualified she exercises this right. As I believe this anomaly to be injurious to the best interests of the country, I trust

to see it removed by the wisdom of Parliament. — Yours sincerely, B. Disraeli."

This was written in 1873 in immediate prospect of the dissolution of Parliament, which took place in February 1874, and placed Mr. Disraeli in power for the first time.

These were days of active propaganda for all the suffrage societies. A hundred meetings were held on the first six months of 1873, a large number for that time, though it would be considered nothing now. All the experienced political men who supported women's suffrage told us that when the 1874 Parliament came to an end a change of Government was highly probable, a new Liberal Government would be in power, and would certainly deal with the question of representation — that then would be the great opportunity, the psychological moment, for the enfranchisement of women. The agricultural labourers were about to be enfranchised and the claim of women to share in the benefits of representative government was at least as good, and would certainly be listened to. With these hopes we approached the election of 1880.

CHAPTER III
THROWING THE WOMEN
OVERBOARD IN 1884

"We have filled the well-fed with good things, and the hungry we have sent empty away." — From the *Politician's Magnificat.*

The year 1880 opened cheerfully for suffragists. There was a series of great demonstrations of women only, beginning with one in the Free Trade Hall, Manchester, in February. The first little bit of practical success too within the United Kingdom came this year, for suffrage was extended to women in the Isle of Man. At first it was given only to women freeholders, but after a few years' experience of its entirely successful operation all feeling of opposition to it died away, and it was extended to women householders. The representative system of the Isle of Man is one of the oldest in the world, and the House of Keys is of even greater antiquity than the House of Commons.

The general election took place in March and April 1880, and the Liberals were returned to power with a large majority. Mr. Gladstone became Prime Minister, and it was well known that the extension of Household Suffrage in the counties would be an important feature in the programme of the new Government. Mr. Goschen declined to join Mr. Gladstone's Government, because he was opposed to the extension of the Parliamentary franchise to the agricultural labourers. It is strange how the whirligig of time brings about its revenges. Mr. Goschen held out to the last against the enfranchisement of the agricultural labourers, but after the election of 1906 he publicly congratulated a meeting of Unionist Free Traders on "the magnificent stand the agricultural labourers had made for Free Trade!" If his counsels had prevailed in 1880, not one of these men would have had a vote and could have made a stand for Free Trade or anything else. But in politics memories are short, and no one reminded Lord Goschen, as he had then became, of his stand against the labourers' vote a few years earlier.

As the time approached when the Government of 1880 would introduce their Bill to extend household suffrage to counties, the exertions of the women's suffragists were redoubled. One of the methods of propaganda adopted was the bringing forward of resolutions favourable to women's suffrage at the meetings and representative gatherings of political associations of both the great parties.

Resolutions favourable to an extension of the Parliamentary suffrage to women were carried at the Parliamentary Reform Congress at Leeds in October 1883, at the National Liberal Federation at Bristol in 1883, at the National Reform Union, Manchester, January 1884, at the

National Union of Conservative Associations (Scotland) at Glasgow in 1887, at the National Union of Conservative and Constitutional Associations' Annual Conference (Oxford) 1887, and so on yearly, or at very frequent intervals, down to the present time.[17]

At the Reform Conference at Leeds in 1883, presided over by Mr. John Morley, and attended by 2000 delegates from all parts of the country, it was moved by Dr. Crosskey of Birmingham, and seconded by Mr. Walter M'Laren, to add to the resolution supporting household suffrage in the counties the following rider: — *"That in the opinion of this meeting, any measure for the extension of the suffrage should confer the franchise on women who, possessing the qualifications which entitle men to vote, have now the right of voting in all matters of local government."*

It was pointed out by Mr. M'Laren (now a member of the House of Commons and one of our most valued supporters) that in the previous session a memorial signed by 110 members of Parliament, of whom the chairman, Mr. John Morley, was one, had been handed to Mr. Gladstone, to the effect that no measure for the extension of the franchise would be satisfactory unless it included women. Mrs. Cobden Unwin and Mrs. Helen Clark, the daughters respectively of Richard Cobden and John Bright, spoke in support of the rider, which was carried by

---

[17] *Record of Women's Suffrage*, p. 190, by Helen Blackburn.

a very large majority. But when the Reform Bill of 1884 came before the House of Commons it was found that the inclusion of women within the Bill had an inexorable opponent in the Prime Minister, Mr. Gladstone. He did not oppose Women's Suffrage in principle. In 1871 he had taken part in a woman's suffrage debate in the House of Commons and had said: —

"So far as I am able to form an opinion of the general tone and opinion of our law in these matters, where the peculiar relations of men and women are concerned, that law does less than justice to women, and great mischief, misery, and scandal result from that state of things in many of the occurrences and events of life.... If it should be found possible to arrange a safe and well-adjusted alteration of the law as to political power, the man who shall attain that object, and who shall see his purpose carried onward to its consequences in a more just arrangement of the provisions of other laws bearing upon the condition and welfare of women, will, in my opinion, be a real benefactor to his country."

It is somewhat difficult to deduce from this statement the condition of the mind from which it proceeded; but it was generally thought to mean that Mr. Gladstone believed that women had suffered practical grievances owing to their exclusion from representation, and that it would be for their benefit and for the welfare of the country if a moderate measure of women's suffrage could be passed into law. When, however, it came to moving a definite amendment to include women in the Reform Bill of 1884, the most vehement opposition was offered by Mr. Gladstone; not indeed even then to the principle of women's suffrage, but to its being added to the Bill before the House. The idea that household suffrage was not democratic had not then been invented. The Prime Minister's line was that the Government had introduced into the Bill "as much as it could safely carry." The unfortunate nautical metaphor was repeated again and again: "Women's suffrage would overweight the ship." "The cargo which the vessel carries is, in our opinion, a cargo as large as she can safely carry." He accordingly threw the women overboard. So different are the traditions of the politician from the heroic traditions of the seaman who, by duty and instinct alike, is always prompted in moments of danger to save the women first.

Comment has been made on the curious ambiguity of the language in which Mr. Gladstone had supported the principle of women's suffrage in 1871. There was no ambiguity in what he said about it in 1884. In language perfectly plain and easily understood he said, "I offer it [Mr. Woodall's Women's Suffrage Amendment] the strongest opposition in my power, and I must disclaim and renounce responsibility for the measure [i.e. the Government Reform Bill] should my honourable friend succeed in inducing the committee to adopt the amendment." This was on June 10, 1884. The decision resulted in a crushing defeat for women's suffrage. The numbers were 271 against Mr. Woodall's amendment to 135 for it. Among the 271 were 104 Liberals who were pledged supporters of suffrage. Three members of the Government, who were known friends of women's suffrage, did not vote at all, but walked out of the House before the division. To one of them Mr. Gladstone wrote the next day pointing out that to abstain from supporting the Government in a critical division was equivalent to a resignation of office. But he added that a crisis in foreign affairs was approaching which might be of the deepest importance to "the character and honour of the country and to the law, the concord and possibly even the peace of Europe. It would be most unfortunate were the minds of men at such a juncture to be disturbed by the resignation of a cabinet minister and of two other gentlemen holding offices of great importance." He, therefore, was proposing to his colleagues that he should be authorised to request the three gentlemen referred to, to do the Government the favour of retaining their respective offices. As they had never resigned them, this petition that they should withdraw their resignation seemed a little superfluous.

The blow to women's suffrage dealt by the defeat of Mr. Woodall's Amendment to the 1884 Reform Bill was a heavy one, and was deeply felt by the whole movement. But though fatal to immediate Parliamentary success, the events of 1884 strengthened our cause in the country. Everything which draws public attention to the subject of representation and to the political helplessness of the unrepresented makes people ask themselves more and more "Why are women excluded?" "If representative government is good for men, why should it be bad for women?" "Why do members of Parliament lightly break their promises to non-voters?" It will be remembered that the Reform Bill of 1884 was not finally passed until late in the autumn. While the final stages of the measure were still pending, the Trades Union Congress meeting at Aberdeen passed a resolution, with only three dissentients, "*That this Congress is strongly of opinion that the franchise should be extended to women rate-payers.*" Thus at that critical juncture the working men's most powerful organisation stood by the women whom the Liberal party had betrayed.

New political forces made their appearance very soon after the passing of the Reform Act of 1884, which have had an almost immeasurable effect in promoting the women's suffrage cause. The Reform Act had contained a provision to render paid canvassing illegal, and in 1883 Sir Henry James (afterwards Lord James of Hereford) had introduced, on behalf of the Government, and carried a very stringent Corrupt Practices Act. Its main feature was to place a definite limit, proportioned to the number of electors in each constituency, upon the authorised expenditure of the candidates. Political agents and party managers had been accustomed to employ a large number of men as paid canvassers, and to perform the great amount of clerical and other drudgery connected with electoral organisation. The law now precluded paid canvassing altogether, and, by limiting the authorised expenditure, severely restrained the number of people who could be employed on ordinary business principles, of so much cash for so much work. But the work had got to be done, or elections would be lost. It was necessary, therefore, to look round and see how and by whom the work could be performed now that the fertilising shower of gold was withdrawn. The brilliant idea occurred to Lord Randolph Churchill, Sir Algernon Borthwick, and others to obtain for their own party the services of ladies. This was the germ of the organisation which soon became known by the name of the Primrose League. Ladies were encouraged to take an active part in the electoral organisation; they canvassed, they spoke, they looked up "removals," and "out voters," and did all kinds of important political work without fee or reward of any kind, and, therefore, without adding to candidates' expenses. The ladies were highly successful from the very first. They showed powers of work and of political organisation which heretofore had been unsuspected. Their political friends were delighted. The anger of their political opponents was unmeasured. It was then that the expression "filthy witches" was used in relation to the Dames of the Primrose League by an excited member of the Liberal party, who attributed his defeat in a contested election to their machinations. But anger quickly gave way to a more practical frame of mind. If the Conservatives could make good use of women for electoral work, Liberals could do so also and would not be left behind. The Women's Liberal Federation[18] was formed in 1886 under the Presidency of Mrs. Gladstone, supported on the executive committee by other ladies, mainly the wives of the Liberal leaders. The idea of the officers of this association from the outset was that the object of its existence was to promote the interests of the Liberal party, or, as Mrs. Gladstone once put it, "to help our husbands." Events, however, soon followed which created great dissatisfaction among the rank and file with this limited range of political activity. There were many women in the association who desired not merely to help their party but to educate it, by promoting Liberal principles, and of these the extension of representative government to women was one of the most important.

The Federation was formed in 1886; the very next year a women's suffrage resolution was moved at the annual council meeting, but was defeated. The same thing happened in 1888 and 1889, the influence of the official Liberal ladies being used against it. In 1890, however, a women's suffrage resolution was carried by a large majority. The earnest suffragists in the Federation continued their work, and in 1892 they became so powerful that fifteen of the members of the executive

---

[18] A few isolated associations of Liberal women had existed before this. There was one at Bristol started in 1881; but nothing was done on an extended scale till 1886.

committee, who had opposed suffrage being taken up as part of the work of the Federation, did not offer themselves for re-election. Mrs. Gladstone, however, did not withdraw, and continued to hold the office of president. The retiring members of the executive took a considerable number of the local associations with them, and in 1893 these formed a new organisation called the National Women's Liberal Association. Some of those who formed this seceding Women's Liberal Association were definitely opposed to Women's Suffrage; others thought that while in principle the enfranchisement of women was right, the time had not come for its practical adoption. In practice, however, the Women's Liberal Federation has stood for suffrage with ever-increasing firmness since 1890, while the Women's Liberal Association has continued to oppose it.

The formation of women's political associations was encouraged by party leaders of all shades of politics. There is probably not a single party leader, however strongly he may oppose the extension of the suffrage to women, who has not encouraged the active participation of women in electoral work. The Liberal party issues a paper of printed directions to those who are asking to do electoral work in its support. The first of these directions is: — *Make all possible use of every available woman in your locality.*

Suffragists contend that a party which can do this cannot long maintain that women are by the mere fact of their sex unfit to be entrusted with a Parliamentary vote.

Even as long ago as his first Midlothian campaign, and before any definite political organisations for women existed, Mr. Gladstone had urged the women of his future constituency to come out and bear their part in the coming electoral struggle. Speaking to a meeting of women in Dalkeith in 1879 he said: —

"Therefore, I think in appealing to you ungrudgingly to open your own feelings and bear your own part in a political crisis like this, we are making no inappropriate demand, but are beseeching you to fulfil the duties which belong to you, which so far from involving any departure from your character as women, are associated with the fulfilment of that character and the performance of those duties, the neglect of which would in future years be a source of pain and mortification, and the accomplishment of which would serve to gild your future years with sweet remembrances and to warrant you in hoping that each in your own place and sphere has raised your voice for justice, and has striven to mitigate the sorrows and misfortunes of mankind."

In less ornate language Mr. Asquith, in January 1910, thanked the women of Fife for the aid they had given him and his cause during the election, and said that "their healthy influence on the masculine members of the community had had not a little to do with keeping things in a satisfactory condition."

The organised political work of women has grown since 1884, and has become so valuable that none of the parties can afford to do without it or to alienate it. Short of the vote itself this is one of the most important political weapons which can possibly have been put into our hands. At the outset, while the women's political societies were still young, and were hardly conscious of their power, the women's suffrage movement benefited greatly by their existence. If the Women's Liberal Federation had existed in 1884, the 104 Liberals who voted against Mr. Woodall's amendment would have probably decided that honesty was the best policy. In 1892 Sir Albert Rollit introduced a Women's Suffrage Bill, as nearly as possible on the lines of the Conciliation Bill of 1910-11. Before the second reading great efforts were made by the Liberal party machine to secure a crushing defeat for this Bill on its second reading: a confidential circular was sent out to all Liberal candidates in the Home Counties advising them not to allow Liberal women to speak on their platforms lest they should advocate "female suffrage." In addition to this, Mr. Gladstone was induced to write a letter addressed to Mr. Samuel Smith, M.P., against the Bill, in which he departed from his previous view that the political work done by women would be quite consistent with womanly character and duties, and would "gild their future years with sweet remembrances." He now said that voting would, he feared, "trespass upon their delicacy, their purity, their refinement, the elevation of their whole nature."

In addition to all this a whip was sent out signed by twenty members of Parliament, ten from each side of the House, earnestly beseeching members to be in their places when Sir Albert Rollit's Bill came on and to vote against the second reading. But when the division came, notwithstanding all the unusual efforts that had been made, it was only defeated by 23. A general election was known to be not very far off, and members who were expecting zealous and efficient support from women in their constituencies did not care to alienate it by denying to women the smallest and most elementary of political privileges. In surprising numbers (as compared with 1884) they stood to their guns, and though they did not save the Bill, the balance against it was so small that it was an earnest of future victory. This division in 1892 was the last time a Women's Suffrage Bill was defeated on a straight issue in the House of Commons. Mr. Faithfull Begg's Bill in 1897 was carried on second reading by 228 votes to 157. After this date direct frontal attacks on the principle of women's suffrage were avoided in the House of Commons. The anti-suffragists in Parliament used every possible trick and stratagem to prevent the subject being discussed and divided on in the House. In this they were greatly helped by Mr. Labouchere, to whom it was a congenial task to shelve the women's suffrage question. On one occasion he and his little group of supporters talked for hours about a Bill dealing with "verminous persons," because it stood before a Suffrage Bill, and he thus succeeded in preventing our Bill from coming before the House.

CHAPTER IV
WOMEN'S SUFFRAGE IN GREATER BRITAIN

"Wake up, Mother Country."
— Speech by King George V. when Prince of Wales.

The debate on Sir Albert Rollit's Bill in 1892 brought out a full display of oratorical power from all quarters of the House, both for and against women's suffrage. Mr. James Bryce, Mr. Asquith, and Sir Henry James (afterwards Lord James) spoke against the Bill. Mr. Balfour, Mr. (now Lord) Courtney, and Mr. Wyndham supported it. When Mr. Bryce spoke he used the timid argument that women's suffrage was an untried experiment. "It is a very bold experiment," he said; "our colonies are democratic in the highest degree; why do they not try it?" and again, "This is an experiment so large and bold that it ought to be tried by some other country first." Mr. Asquith, in the course of his speech, said much the same thing: "We have no experience to guide us one way or the other." Mr. Goldwin Smith, an extra-Parliamentary opponent of women's suffrage, pointed, in an article, to its solitary example in the State of Wyoming, where it had been adopted in 1869, and asked why, if suffrage had been a success in Wyoming, its example had not been followed by other states immediately abutting on its borders.

Now it has frequently been noticed that when this line of argument is adopted it seems to be a sort of "mascot" for women's suffrage. When Mr. Bryce inquired in 1892 "why our great democratic colonies had not tried women's suffrage," his speech was followed in 1893 by the adoption of women's suffrage in New Zealand and in South Australia. When Mr. Goldwin Smith asked why the States which were in nearest neighbourhood to Wyoming had not followed her example, three States in this position, namely Colorado in 1893, Utah in 1895, and Idaho in 1896, very rapidly did so. When Sir F. S. Powell, in 1907, said in the House of Commons that no country in Europe had ever ventured on the dangerous experiment of enfranchising its women, women's suffrage was granted in Finland the same year, and in Norway the year following. When Mrs. Humphry Ward wrote in 1908 that our cause in the United States was "in process of defeat and extinction," this was followed by the most important suffrage victories ever won in America — the States of Washington in 1910, and California in 1911.

The question arises why so well informed and careful a political controversialist as Mr. James Bryce spoke as he did in 1892 of the fact that none of our great democratic colonies had adopted women's suffrage, in evident ignorance of the fact that two at any rate were on the point of doing so. The answer is probably to be found in the attitude of the anti-suffrage press. No body of political controversialists are so badly served by their own press as the anti-suffragists. The anti-suffrage press appears to act on the assumption that if they say nothing about a political event it is the same as if it had not happened. Therefore, while they give prominence to any circumstances which they imagine likely to be injurious to suffrage, they either say nothing about those facts which indicate its growing force and volume, or record them in such a manner that they escape the observation of the general reader. The result is that only the suffragists, who are in constant communication with their comrades in various parts of the world and also have their own papers, are kept duly informed, not only of what has happened, but of what is likely to happen. Mr. Bryce cannot have known of the imminence of the success of women's suffrage in New Zealand and South Australia in 1892. Mrs. Humphry Ward did not know in February 1909 that women's suffrage had actually been carried in Victoria, and had received the royal assent in 1908. She could have known very little of the real strength of the suffrage movement in the United States, when she said it was virtually dead, just at the moment when it was about to give the most unmistakable proofs of energy and vigour. For all this ignorance the anti-suffrage press of London is mainly responsible. "Things are what they are and their consequences will be what they will be," whether the newspapers print them or not, and to leave the controversialists on your own side in ignorance of facts of capital importance is a strange way of showing political allegiance.[19]

It is a mistake to represent that women's suffrage was brought about in New Zealand suddenly or, as it were, by accident. The women of New Zealand did not, as has sometimes been said, wake up one fine morning in 1893 and find themselves enfranchised. Sustained, self-sacrificing, painstaking, and well-organised work for women's suffrage had been going on in the Colony for many years.[20] The germ of it may be traced even as early as 1843, and many of the most distinguished men whose names are connected with New Zealand history as true empire-builders have been identified with the movement, including Mr. John Ballance, Sir Julius Vogel, Sir R. Stout, Sir John Hall, and Sir George Grey. It is curious that Mr. Richard Seddon, under whose Premiership women's suffrage was finally carried, was not at that time (1893) a believer in it. He was a Thomas who had to see before he could believe, but when he had once had experience of women's suffrage, he was unwearied in proclaiming his confidence in it. When he was in England in 1902 for King

---

[19] An important new departure in journalism was taken by *The Standard* in October 1911. This paper now devotes more than a page daily to a full statement both of events and arguments bearing on all sides of the suffrage and other women's questions.

[20] See *Outlines of the Women's Franchise Movement in New Zealand*, by W. Sydney Smith. Whitecombe & Tombs, Ltd., Christchurch, N.Z. 1905.

Edward's Coronation he hardly ever spoke in public without bearing his testimony to the success of women's suffrage. Much good seed had been sown in New Zealand by Mrs. Müller, an English lady, who landed in Nelson in 1850. One of her articles, signed "Femina" (she was obliged to preserve her anonymity for reasons of domestic tranquillity), won the attention of John Stuart Mill, and drew from him a most encouraging letter, and the gift of his book *The Subjection of Women*. Mrs. Müller died in 1902, and thus had the opportunity of seeing in operation for nearly ten years the successful operation of the reform for which she had been one of the earliest workers. An American lady, Mrs. Mary Clement Leavitt, visited New Zealand in 1885 on behalf of the Women's Christian Temperance Union. Mrs. Leavitt was a great organiser and arranged the whole of the work of the Temperance Union in definite "Departments," and a general superintendent was appointed to each. There was a Franchise Department, the general superintendent of which was Mrs. Sheppard, who, from 1887, became an indefatigable and, at the same time, a cautious and sensible worker for the extension of the Parliamentary franchise to women. She was in communication with Sir John Hall and other Parliamentary leaders, and kept in close touch with the whole movement until it was successful.

Just as it is now in England with us, differences arose among New Zealand suffragists as to how much suffrage women ought to have, or at any rate for how much would it be wise to ask, and the parties were called the "half loafers" and the "whole loafers." The "no bread" party watched these differences just as they do in England, and tried unsuccessfully to profit by them. In the debate on Sir John Hall's Women's Suffrage resolution in 1890, Mr. W. P. Reeves, so long known in England as the Agent-General for New Zealand, and later as the Director of the London School of Economics, and also as an excellent friend of women's suffrage, announced himself to be a "half loafer"; indeed he advocated the restriction of the franchise to such women, over twenty-one years of age, who had passed the matriculation examination of the university. There is an Arabic proverb to the effect that the world is divided into three classes — "the immovable, the movable, and those who actually move." It is unwise to despair of the conversion of any anti-suffragist unless he has proved himself to belong to the "immovables." In 1890 Mr. Reeves, now so good a suffragist, had only advanced to the point of advocating the enfranchisement of university women. His proposal for a high educational suffrage test for women did not meet with support. It was rejected by more robust suffragists as "not even half a loaf, only a ginger nut." The anti-suffragists used the same arguments which they use with us. They professed themselves to be intimately acquainted with the views of the Almighty on the question of women voting. "It was contrary to the ordinance of God"; women politicians were represented as driving a man from his home because it would be infested "with noisy and declamatory women." After the Bill had passed both Houses a solemn petition was presented by anti-suffragists, who were members of the Legislative Council, asking the Governor to withhold his assent on the ground that "it would seriously affect the rights of property and embarrass the finances of the colony, thereby injuriously affecting the public creditor." Others protested that it was self-evident, that women's suffrage must lead to domestic discord and the neglect of home life. Of course all the anti-suffragists were certain that women did not want the vote, and would not use it even if it were granted to them.

The French gentleman who called himself Max O'Rell was touring New Zealand at the time, and deplored that one of the fairest spots on God's earth was going to be turned into a howling wilderness by women's suffrage. Mr. Goldwin Smith wrote that he gave women's suffrage ten years in New Zealand, and by that time it would have wrought such havoc with the home and domestic life that the best minds in the country would be devising means of getting rid of it. A New Zealand gentleman, named Bakewell, wrote an article in *The Nineteenth Century* for February 1894, containing a terrible jeremiad about the melancholy results to be expected in the Dominion from women's suffrage. The last words of his article were, "We shall probably for some years to come be a dreadful object lesson to the rest of the British Empire." This was the prophecy. What have the facts been? New Zealand has become an object-lesson — an object-lesson of faithful membership of the Imperial group, a daughter State of which the mother country is intensely proud. Does not everybody know that New Zealand is prosperous and happy and loyal to the throne and race to which she owes her origin.[21] New Zealand was the first British Colony to enfranchise her women, and was also the first British Colony to send her sons to stand side by side with the sons of Great Britain in the battlefields of South Africa; she was also the first British Colony to cable the offer of a battleship to the mother country in the spring of 1909. She, with Australia, was the first part of the British Empire to devise and carry out a truly national system of defence, seeking the advice of the first military expert of the mother country, Lord Kitchener, to help them to do it on efficient lines. The women are demanding that they should do their share in the great national work of defence by undergoing universal ambulance training.[22]

New Zealand and Australia have, since they adopted women's suffrage, inaugurated many important social and economic reforms, among which may be mentioned wages boards — the principle of the minimum wage applied to women as well as to men — and the establishment of

---

[21] See Report by Sir Charles Lucas, who visited New Zealand on behalf of the Colonial Office in 1907.

[22] See *Colonial Statesmen and Votes for Women*, published by The Freedom League, p. 6.

children's courts for juvenile offenders. They have also purged their laws of some of the worst of the enactments injurious to women. If it were needed to rebut the preposterous nonsense urged by anti-suffragists against women's suffrage in New Zealand eighteen years ago, it is sufficient to quote the unemotional terms of the cable which appeared from New Zealand in *The Times* of July 28, 1911: —

"Parliament was opened to-day. Lord Islington, the Governor, in his speech, congratulated the Dominion on its continued prosperity. The increase in the material well-being of the people, was, he said, encouraging, and there was every reason to expect a continuance and even an augmentation of the prosperity of the trade and industry of the Dominion.... The results of registration under the universal defence training scheme were satisfactory. The spirit in which this call for patriotism had been met was highly commendable."

The testimony concerning the practical working of women's suffrage in Australia and New Zealand is all of one kind. It may be summarised in a single sentence, "Not one of the evils so confidently predicted of it has actually happened." The effect on home life is universally said to have been good. The birth-rate in New Zealand has steadily increased since 1899, and it has now, next to Australia, the lowest infantile mortality in the world. In South Australia, where women have been enfranchised since 1893, the infantile death-rate has also been reduced from 130 in the 1000 to half that number. Our own anti-suffragists are quite capable of representing that this argument means that we are so foolish as to suppose that if a mother drops a paper into a ballot-box every few years she thereby prolongs the life of her infant. Of course we do nothing of the kind; but we do say that to give full citizenship to women deepens in them the sense of responsibility, and they will be more likely to apply to their duties a quickened intelligence and a higher sense of the importance of the work entrusted to them as women. The free woman makes the best wife and the most careful mother.

The confident prediction that women when enfranchised would not take the trouble to record their votes has been falsified. The men and women who were on the electoral roll voted in almost the same proportion. The number of votes actually polled compared with the number on the register is, of course, to some extent affected by the number of constituencies in which there is no contest, or in which the result is regarded as a foregone conclusion; but this consideration affects both sexes alike. It is impossible for reasons of space to enter in detail in this little book upon the history in each of the Australian States of the adoption of women's suffrage. But it is well known that every one of the States forming the Commonwealth of Australia has now enfranchised its women, and that one of the first acts of the Commonwealth Parliament in 1902 was to grant the suffrage to women. The complete list of dates of women's enfranchisement in New Zealand and Australia will be found in *The Brief Review of the Women's Suffrage Movement*.

When the Premiers and other political leaders from the overseas Dominions of Great Britain were in London for the Coronation and Imperial Conference of 1911, the representatives of Australia and New Zealand frequently expressed both in public and in private their entire satisfaction with the results of women's suffrage. Mr. Fisher, the Premier of the Commonwealth, constantly spoke in this sense: "There is no Australian politician who would nowadays dare to get up at a meeting and declare himself an enemy.... It has had most beneficial results.... He had not the slightest doubt that women's votes had had a good effect on social legislation.... The Federal Parliament took a strong stand upon the remuneration of women, and the minimum wage which was laid down applied equally to women and men for the same work" (*Manchester Guardian* June 3, 1911). On another occasion Mr. Fisher said that so far from women's suffrage causing any disunion between men and women, "the interest which men took in women's affairs when women had got the vote was wonderful" (*Manchester Guardian* June 10, 1911). Sir William Lyne, Premier of New South Wales, said: "When the women were enfranchised in Australia they proceeded at each election to purify their Parliament, and they had gone on doing so, and now he was proud to say their Parliament was one of the model Parliaments of the world" (*Manchester Guardian* August 1, 1911). The Hon. John Murray of Victoria and the Hon. A. A. Kirkpatrick spoke in the same sense. Indeed the evidence favourable to the working of women's suffrage is overwhelming, and is given not only by men who have always supported it, but by those who formerly opposed it, and have had the courage to acknowledge that as the result of experience they have changed their views. Among these may be mentioned Sir Edmund Barton, the first Premier of the Commonwealth, and the late Sir Thomas Bent, the Premier of Victoria, under whose administration women were enfranchised in that State. Why appeal to other witnesses when both Houses of the Commonwealth Parliament in November 1910 unanimously adopted the following resolution: —

"(i.) That this [House / Senate] is of opinion that the extension of the Suffrage to the women of Australia for States and Commonwealth Parliaments, on the same terms as men, has had the most beneficial results. It has led to the more orderly conduct of Elections, and at the last Federal Elections the women's vote in the majority of the States showed a greater proportionate increase than that cast by men. It has given a greater prominence to legislation particularly affecting women and children, although the women have not taken up such questions to the exclusion of others of wider significance. In matters of Defence and Imperial concern, they have proved themselves as far-seeing and discriminating as men.

Because the reform has brought nothing but good, though disaster was freely prophesied, we respectfully urge that all Nations enjoying Representative Government would be well advised in granting votes to women."

With all this wealth of testimony rebutting from practical experience almost every objection urged against women's suffrage, it is impossible to exaggerate the value to the movement here of the example of Australia and New Zealand. There are few families in the United Kingdom that have not ties of kindred or of friendship with Australasia. The men and women there are of our own race and traditions, starting from the same stock, owning the same allegiance, acknowledging the same laws, speaking the same language, nourished mentally, morally, and spiritually from the same sources. We visit them and they visit us; and when their women return to what they fondly term "home," although they may have been born and brought up under the Southern Cross, they naturally ask why they should be put into a lower political status in Great Britain than in the land of their birth? What have they done to lose one of the most elementary guarantees of liberty and citizenship? As the ties of a sane and healthy Imperialism draw us closer together the difference in the political status of women in Great Britain and her daughter States will become increasingly indefensible and cannot be long maintained.

CHAPTER V
The Anti-Suffragists

"We enjoy every species of indulgence we can wish for;
and as we are content, we pray that others who are not
content may meet with no relief."
— Burke in House of Commons in 1772 on the
Dissenters who petitioned against Dissenters.

The first organised opposition by women to women's
suffrage in England dates from 1889, when a number of
ladies, led by Mrs. Humphry Ward, Miss Beatrice Potter
(now Mrs. Sidney Webb), and Mrs. Creighton appealed in
The Nineteenth Century against the proposed extension of
the Parliamentary suffrage to women. Looking back now
over the years that have passed since this protest was
published, the first thing that strikes the reader is that some
of the most distinguished ladies who then co-operated with
Mrs. Humphry Ward have ceased to be anti-suffragists,
and have become suffragists. Mrs. Creighton and Mrs.
Webb have joined us; they are not only "movable," but
they have moved, and have given their reasons for
changing their views. Turning from the list of names to the
line of argument adopted against women's suffrage, we

find, on the contrary, no change, no development. The ladies who signed *The Nineteenth Century* protest in 1889 were then as now — and this is the essential characteristic of the anti-suffrage movement — completely in favour of every improvement in the personal, proprietary, and political status of women that had already been gained, *but against any further extension of it. The Nineteenth Century* ladies were in 1889 quite in favour of women taking part in all local government elections, for women's right to do this had been won in 1870. The protesting ladies said in so many words *"we believe the emancipating process has now reached the limits fixed by the physical constitution of women."* Less wise than Canute, they appeared to think they could order the tide of human progress to stop and that their command would be obeyed. Then, as now, they protested that the normal experience of women "does not, and never can, provide them with such material to form a sound judgment on great political affairs as men possess," or, as Mrs. Humphry Ward has more recently expressed it, "the political ignorance of women is irreparable and is imposed by nature"; then having proclaimed the inherent incapacity of women to form a sound judgment on important political affairs, they proceed to formulate a judgment on one of the most important issues of practical politics. Several of the ladies who signed *The Nineteenth Century* protest in 1889 were at that moment taking an active part in organising the political work and influence of women for or against the main political issue of the day, the granting of Home Rule to Ireland; and yet they were saying at the same time that women had not the material to form a sound judgment in politics. This is, of course, the inherent absurdity of the whole position of anti-suffrage women. If women are incapable of forming a sound judgment in grave political issues, why invite them and urge them to express an opinion at all? Besides this fundamental absurdity there is another, secondary to it, but none the less real. Anti-suffragists, especially anti-suffrage men, maintain that to take part in the strife and turmoil of practical politics is in its essence degrading to women, and calculated to sully their refinement and purity. If this, indeed, is so, why invite women into the turmoil? Why advertise, as the anti-suffragists do, the holding of classes to train young women to become anti-suffrage speakers, and thus be able to proclaim on public platforms that "woman's place is home?" This second absurdity appears to have occurred to the late editor of *The Nineteenth Century*, Sir James Knowles, for a note is added to the 1889 protest apologising, as it were, for the inconsistency of asking women to degrade themselves by taking part in a public political controversy: —

"It is submitted," says this note, "that for once and in order to save the quiet of Home Life from total disappearance they should do violence to their natural reticence and signify publicly and unmistakably their condemnation of the scheme now threatened."

If this note was, as it appears, by the editor, how much he, too, needed the lesson which Canute gave to his courtiers. The waves were not to be turned back by a hundred and odd great ladies doing violence to their natural reticence and signifying publicly that they were very well satisfied with things as they were. "Just for once, in order to save the quiet of home life from total disappearance," these milk white lambs, bleating for man's protection, were to cast aside their timidity and come before the public with a protest against a further extension of human liberty. The anti-suffrage protest of 1889 had the effect which similar protests have ever since had of adding to the numbers and the activity of the suffragists.

Women anti-suffragists formed themselves into a society in July 1908 under the leadership of Mrs. Humphry Ward, and a men's society was shortly afterwards formed under the chairmanship of the Earl of Cromer. These two societies were amalgamated in December 1910. Lord Cromer is the President, and exerts himself actively in opposition to women's suffrage, and in obtaining funds for the League of which he is the leader. In the previous spring of 1910 the Anti-Suffrage League had adopted as part of its programme, besides the negative object of opposing women's suffrage, the positive object of encouraging "the principle of the representation of women on municipal and other bodies concerned with the domestic and social affairs of the community." But male anti-suffragists dwell chiefly on the negative part of their programme. As a fairly regular reader of the *Anti-Suffrage Review* I may say that the advocacy of municipal suffrage and eligibility for women bears about the same proportion to the anti-suffrage part of it as Falstaff's bread did to his sack; it is always one halfpennyworth of bread, and even that is sometimes absent, to an intolerable deal of sack.

The English anti-suffragists' combination of opposing Parliamentary suffrage and supporting municipal suffrage for women has no counterpart in the United States. American anti-suffragists are as bitterly opposed to municipal and school suffrage for women (where it does not exist) as they are to political suffrage. In the State of New York, not many years ago, the Albany Association for Opposing Woman's Suffrage vehemently resisted the appointment of women on School Boards and said, "It threatens the home, threatens the sacredness of the marriage tie, threatens the Church, and undermines the constitution of our great Republic." An American senator, not to be outdone, improved even upon this, and spoke of school suffrage for women in Massachusetts in the following terms: "If we make this experiment we shall destroy the race which will be blasted by the vengeance of Almighty God." These extravagances do not belong entirely to the dark ages of the nineteenth century; only in the summer of 1911 the *New York Association opposed to the extension of the suffrage to women* successfully opposed a Bill to confer the municipal suffrage on women in Connecticut. This Bill had passed the Senate and was before the House of Representatives, which was immediately besieged by petitions against the Bill urging all the old arguments with which we are so familiar in this country against the Parliamentary suffrage, such as that it was not fair to women that they should have the municipal vote "thrust upon them"; that Governments rest on force, and force is male; that women cannot fight, and therefore should not vote; that to give the municipal vote to women would destroy the home, and undermine the foundations of society.[23]

This opposition was successful, and the Bill was defeated in face of overwhelming evidence derived from the numerous cases which were quoted of women exercising the municipal vote, and sitting as members of local governing bodies without producing any of the disastrous consequences so confidently predicted. Where women have the municipal vote there is no opposition to it in any quarter, because it is overwhelmingly evident, as Mr. Gladstone once said, that "it has been productive of much good and no harm whatever."

English suffragists can only heartily rejoice that English anti-suffragists are so much more intelligent than those of the United States. It shows that they are capable of learning from experience. Women have had the municipal vote in Great Britain since 1870, and they have voted for

---

[23] See letter from Miss Alice Stone Blackwell in *Manchester Guardian*, July 12, 1911

Poor Law Guardians and School Boards (where such still exist) from the same date. They were rendered eligible for Town and County Councils in 1907 by an Act passed by Sir Henry Campbell Bannerman's Government. Suffragists are far from complaining that anti-suffragists rejoice with them at these extensions of civic liberty to women. Though the battle is over and the victory won, it is very satisfactory to see the good results of women's suffrage, where it exists, recognised and emphasised even by anti-suffragists. Mrs. Humphry Ward has advocated the systematic organisation of the women's vote in London local elections in order to have increased motive power behind some of her excellent schemes for making more use of playgrounds for the benefit of the London children. She has also spoken several times in public in favour of the increased representation of women on local government bodies; and has even gone very near to making a joke on the subject, saying, in justification of her attitude, "That it was not good to allow the devil to have all the best tunes," and not wise for the anti-suffragists to allow the suffragists to claim a monopoly of ideas and enthusiasm.[24]

Still it is rather significant that she comes to the suffrage camp for the ideas and enthusiasms. Her male colleagues have not shown themselves very ardent in the cause of equal rights for women in local government. In 1898,

---

[24] See *Anti-Suffrage Review*, No. 33, p. 167

when the London Borough Councils were established in the place of the Vestries, an amendment was moved and carried in the House of Commons rendering women eligible for the newly created bodies as they had been on the old ones. When the Bill came to the House of Lords, this portion of it was vehemently opposed by the late Lord James of Hereford (afterwards one of the vice-presidents of the Anti-Suffrage League), and his opposition was successful, notwithstanding a powerful and eloquent speech by the late Lord Salisbury, then Prime Minister, in support of the eligibility of women on the new Borough Councils. Again, when in 1907 the Bill rendering women eligible for Town and County Councils reached the House of Lords, it had no more sincere and ardent opponent than Lord James. He saw its bearing upon the question of women's suffrage, and the absurdity involved in a state of the law which allows a woman to be a Town or County Councillor, or even a Mayor, and in that capacity the returning officer at a Parliamentary election, but does not permit her to give a simple vote in the election of a member of Parliament.

"If," said Lord James, "their Lordships accepted this measure making women eligible for the great positions that had been specified in great communities like Liverpool and Manchester, *where was the man who would be able to argue against the Parliamentary franchise for women?*"

The Bill became an Act, notwithstanding Lord James's opposition, and within twelve months he had become a vice-president of the League for Opposing Women's Suffrage and for "Maintaining the Representation of Women on Municipal and other Bodies concerned with the Domestic and Social Affairs of the Community."

It has been said by Mrs. Humphry Ward, Miss Violet Markham, and other anti-suffragists that it is not very creditable to women's public spirit that four years after the passing of the Local Government Qualification of Women Act of 1907, so few women[25] are serving on Town and County Councils. The chief reason for their insignificant numbers is that at present only those women may be elected who are themselves qualified to elect. Outside London this disqualifies married women, and in London it only qualifies those married women who are on the register as municipal voters. It also disqualifies daughters living, under normal conditions, in the houses of their parents. The range of choice of women candidates is, therefore, very severely restricted. Similar disqualifications in former years applied to the post of Poor Law Guardian. When a simple residential qualification was substituted for the electoral qualification the number of women acting as Poor Law Guardians increased in a few years from about 160 to over 1300, of

---

[25] The exact numbers in England and Wales (autumn 1911) are fifteen on Town Councils (two being Mayors) and four on County Councils.

whom eight out of nine have the residential qualification only, nearly half of them being married women. It helps people to realise how the present law limits the range of choice of women to serve on locally elected bodies to ask them to consider what would be the effect on the number of men who could offer themselves for election if marriage were a disqualification for them also. A Bill for allowing women to be elected to Town and County Councils on a residential qualification has been before Parliament for the four sessions 1908-11. It is "non-contentious," but it has never even got a second reading. Bills concerning women lack the motive power behind them which is almost invariably necessary for the successful passage of a Bill through all its stages. Mrs. Humphry Ward and Miss Markham have some justification for their contention that the suffrage movement has largely absorbed the energies of the more active-minded women, and prevented them from offering themselves as candidates in municipal elections. This is inevitable. Not everyone possesses the boundless energy of such women as Miss Margaret Ashton, Miss Eleanor Rathbone, or Mrs. Lees, who combine active suffrage propaganda with work of first-class importance as members of councils in large and important towns. But when once the battle for suffrage is won, and the qualification is made reasonable for women, it is almost certain that the number of women elected on municipal bodies will largely increase. In Norway, where women's suffrage has been in operation since 1908, although the population is only a little over 2,000,000, the number of women elected on Town and County Councils in 1911 was 210, and as many as 379 have been elected in addition as "alternates." It appears, therefore, that the secondary object of the Anti-Suffrage League, "the representation of women on municipal bodies," would be best served by extending the Parliamentary franchise to women.

The Anti-Suffrage League in England has made a great point of the number of petitions and protests which they have obtained from women municipal voters declaring their antagonism to women's suffrage in Parliamentary elections. The suffragists, however, attach little or no importance to the figures which have been published. When suffragists conduct a canvass of the same people on the same subject the result is entirely different. Much criticism has been made upon the manner in which the anti-suffragists have obtained the signatures to their petitions and protests against women's suffrage, and we know that in some cases signatures have been asked for "as a protest against being governed by these lawless women." Now there are almost as many fallacies in this sentence as there are words. Many ardent suffragists, probably the majority of them, are opposed to the use of physical violence as a means of obtaining political justice. Moreover, women are not lawless. Women in this country, as all criminal statistics prove, are about nine times more law-abiding than men.[26] If people object to being governed by the more lawless sex, it is not women who should be disfranchised. And besides these considerations there is another — the voter, whether male or female, does not govern. He, when he gives his vote, has to decide between two or more men representing different sets of principles, to which he wishes to confide the various tasks of government.

The *Anti-Suffrage Review* of January 1911 contained an article called "Arguments for use in Poor Districts," which throws a flood of light on the methods by which these signatures of women against women's suffrage have been obtained. The article represents an anti-suffrage lady going round with a petition against women's suffrage. She approaches the house of a working woman and appeals to her whether, after she has looked after her children and her home, she has not done all that a woman has time for, and "had better leave such things as the Government of India and the Army and Navy, and all those outside things to the men who understand them." A more extraordinarily dishonest argument, if argument it can be called, can hardly be imagined. If it were sound, it would exclude from all share in political power not only working women, but also working men — all who live by the sweat of their brow, and all hard working professional and business men. If the argument were a sound one, the best Government

---

[26] See Statistical Abstract from the United Kingdom.

would be a bureaucracy like that of Russia, where the great tasks of government and the management of the Army and Navy "are left to the men who understand them," and where the peasant, the artisan, the professional man, and the merchant have nothing to do with laws but to obey them, and nothing to do with taxes but to pay them. But this system has never commended itself to the political instincts of the British nation. Some of the anti-suffragists at any rate could see this plainly enough when this "argument" was applied to the continued exclusion of working men from the franchise. Mr. Frederic Harrison has written words on this very subject which are as applicable to women today as they were to men at the time when they were first published: —

"Electors have not got to govern a country; they have only to find a set of men who will see that the Government is fresh and active.... Government is one thing, but electors of any class cannot and ought not to govern. Electing, or giving an indirect approval of Government, is another thing, and demands wholly different qualities. These are moral, not intellectual, practical, not special gifts — gifts of a very plain and almost universal order. Such are, firstly, social sympathies and sense of justice, then openness and plainness of character; lastly, habits of action and a practical knowledge of social misery "[27]

---

[27] Quoted in Lord Morley's *Studies in Literature*, pp. 133, 134. The reference there given for the extract is *Order and Progress*, by Frederic Harrison, pp. 149-154.

These are the lessons of their own leaders; but the anti-suffragists pay no heed to them; it is little wonder then that they pay no heed to the great suffrage leader who has taught us that women, like men, do not need the franchise in order that they may govern, but in order that they may not be misgoverned.

One other consideration may be deduced from this extraordinary article — "Arguments for use in Poor Districts." If the anti-suffragists will put into cold print such "arguments" that women ought not to vote because they are occupied with the daily tasks of ordinary life and are not prepared to govern India or manage the Army and Navy, what may not the anti-suffragists say in private in the cottages which they visit in order to overcome the reluctance of working women to put their names to the anti-suffrage petitions?

The women who petition against women's enfranchisement are a type that we have always with us. Burke held them up to disdain and contempt in inimitable words in 1772, when Dissenters petitioned against Dissenters. The Five Mile Act and the Test and Corporation Act were then in force. The Test Act made the taking of the Sacrament according to the rites of the Church of England a necessary qualification for holding public office of any kind. The Five Mile Act forbade the proscribed Nonconformists from preaching or holding meetings within five miles of any corporate town. In 1772 these Acts were not often put into operation, but as long as they were in the Statute Book the Nonconformist leaders felt that they were doomed to live on sufferance; their friends in Parliament prepared a Bill for their relief from these outrageous disabilities. Opposition was, of course, at once awakened; it proceeded mainly from the King and the "King's friends." Their hands were strengthened by receiving a petition signed by dissenting ministers, who entreated Parliament not to surrender a test "imposed expressly for the maintenance of those essential doctrines upon which the Reformation was founded." They were for the time successful, but Burke's oratory has pointed the finger of scorn at them for all time. "Two bodies of men," he said, "approach our House and prostrate themselves at our Bar. 'We ask not honours,' say the one. 'We have no aspiring wishes, no views upon the purple....' 'We, on the contrary,' say the Dissenters who petition against Dissenters, 'enjoy every species of indulgence we can wish for; and as we are content, we pray that others who are not content may meet with no relief.'"[28]

We do not envy the Dissenters who petitioned against Dissenters in the eighteenth century, and future generations will probably mete out no very kindly judgment to the women who petitioned against women in 1889 and 1911: "As we are content, we pray that others who are not content may meet with no relief"

---

[28] *Early History of Charles James Fox,* by the Rt. Hon. Sir G. O. Trevelyan, p. 449.

One most effective reply has been made by the suffragists to the allegation of their opponents that women do not desire their own enfranchisement. Between the autumns of 1910 and 1911 more than 130 local councils petitioned Parliament in favour of passing without delay the Women's Suffrage Bill, known as the Conciliation Bill. These councils comprise those of the most important towns in the kingdom, including Edinburgh, Glasgow, Dundee, Inverness, Dublin, Cork, Limerick, Liverpool, Manchester, Birmingham, Sheffield, Bradford, Oldham, Leeds, Wolverhampton, Newcastle, and Brighton. No such series of petitions from locally elected bodies has probably ever been presented to Parliament in favour of a Franchise Bill. The anti-suffragists have endeavoured to belittle the significance of these petitions. In an important official letter to Mr. Asquith, signed by Lord Cromer, Lady Jersey, Mrs. Humphry Ward, Lord Curzon, and others, it is stated:
—

"The councils which have allowed these resolutions to go through are, in no small degree, dependent for votes upon the very women whom the Bill proposes to enfranchise, *and it is most natural that the councillors should shrink from the risk of offending them.*"[29]

This is a good specimen of anti-suffrage logic. Women householders are strongly opposed to their own enfranchisement; but Town Councillors who depend upon

---

[29] *Anti-Suffrage Review*, December 1910.

the votes of these women are forced to petition in favour of their enfranchisement because these councillors "shrink from the risk of offending them."

It is true that Lord Cromer, Lord Curzon, and the other signatories of the letter go on to say that they are much better acquainted with the feeling of the women municipal voters in the various towns than the men are who have lived in them all their lives, and have repeatedly stood in them as candidates in municipal elections. This illustrates the degree of knowledge possessed by the most distinguished of the anti-suffragists of the work-a-day world in which humbler mortals have to live.

Mr. Gladstone said of the House of Lords when they opposed the Reform Bill of 1884 that they "lived in a balloon," unconscious of what was happening among the dim common populations living on the earth. The same criticism is applicable to the anti-suffragists. They opened the year 1911 in their *Review* by saying that they looked "forward with complete confidence to the work of saving women from the immeasurable injury of having their sex brought into the conflict of political life." This was immediately after the election of December 1910, during which Mrs. Humphry Ward had taken an active personal share in her son's electoral contest in West Hertfordshire; and during which a large number of Unionist candidates and others had had the offer from her publishers of her *Letters to my Friends and Neighbours*, written anew for the second election of 1910, price 3d. each or 1000 copies for £5. No suffragist blames Mrs. Humphry Ward for her active interest in politics. Whether people like it or not, women are taking part in active political work; but to talk of "the immeasurable injury of bringing their sex into the conflict of political life," and at the same time to profit by the political knowledge and enthusiasm of women is a practical absurdity. All parties are alike in getting as much work as possible during an election out of the women who sympathise with them.

To encourage the political activity of women and at the same time talk about "protecting women from the immeasurable injury of having their sex brought into the conflict of political life," helps one to understand why Frenchmen say that the English are a nation of hypocrites.

Some eminent anti-suffragists attacked the Insurance Bill (1911) on the ground that it is "cruelly unfair" to women; others, including some of their most distinguished women, but no men, sent to the Prime Minister in July a carefully worded and powerfully reasoned letter explaining in detail the points in which they felt that the Bill did less than justice to women. Space does not permit a detailed examination of the points raised in this excellent letter, but one sentence in it must be given, for it contains within itself the gist of the case for women's suffrage: —

"We would strongly urge that instead of meeting these and similar cases by amending the Bill in the way which was promised by the Chancellor of the Exchequer on July

10th, *it would be preferable to substitute the insurance which is needed for that which is not needed.*"

The unrepresented are always liable to be given what they do not need rather than what they do need. This, in one sentence, forms the strength of the case for women's suffrage. However benevolent men may be in their intentions, they cannot know what women want and what suits the necessities of women's lives as well as women know these things themselves.

CHAPTER VI
THE MILITANT SOCIETIES

"It is a calumny on men to say that they are roused to
heroic action by ease, hope of pleasure — sugar plums of
any kind. In the meanest mortal there lies something
nobler. Difficulty, abnegation, martyrdom, death, are the
allurements which act upon the heart of man."
— Thomas Carlyle

In Chapters II. and III. an outline was given of the
Parliamentary history of women's suffrage between 1867
and 1897. In those thirty years the movement had
progressed until it had reached a point when it could count
upon a majority of suffragists being returned in each
successively elected House of Commons. In 1899 came
the South African War, and the main interest of the nation
was concentrated on that struggle till it was over. A war
almost invariably suspends all progress in domestic and
social legislation. Two fires cannot burn together, and the
most ardent of the suffragists felt that, while the war
lasted, it was not a fitting time to press their own claims
and objects. The war temporarily suspended the progress
of the suffrage movement, but it is probable that it

ultimately strengthened the demand of women for citizenship, for it has been observed again and again that a war, or any other event which stimulates national vitality, and the consciousness of the value of citizenship is almost certain to be followed by increased vigour in the suffrage movement, and not infrequently by its success. For instance, suffrage in Finland in 1907 followed immediately upon the great struggle with Russia to regain constitutional liberty; women as well as men had thrown themselves into that struggle and borne the great sacrifices it entailed, and when Finland wrung from the Czar the granting of the Constitution, women's suffrage formed an essential part of it, and was demanded by the almost unanimous voice of the Finnish people. Again, when suffrage was granted to women in Norway in 1907, it was immediately after the great outburst of national feeling which led to the separation from Sweden, and established Norway as an independent kingdom. Upon the rights and wrongs of the controversy between the two countries it is not for us to enter, but the intensity of the feeling in Norway in favour of separation is undoubted. The women had shared in the national fervour and in all the work and sacrifices it entailed. The Parliamentary Suffrage was granted to women as one of the first Acts of the Norwegian Parliament.

In the Commonwealth of Australia almost the first Act of the first Parliament was the enfranchisement of women. The national feeling of Australia had been stimulated and the sense of national responsibility deepened by the events which led to the Federation of the Independent States of the Australian Continent. It is true that South Australia and Western Australia had led the way about women's suffrage before this in 1893 and 1899, but up to the time of the formation of the Commonwealth there had been no such rapid extension of the suffrage to women as that which accompanied or immediately followed it.

The fight for suffrage in the United Kingdom is not won yet, but it has made enormous progress towards victory, and this, in my opinion, is in part due to the quickened sense of national responsibility, the deeper sense of the value of citizenship which was created by the South African War. The war in the first instance originated from the refusal of the vote to Englishmen and other "Uitlanders" long settled in the Transvaal. The newspapers, therefore, both in this country and in South Africa constantly dwelt on the value and significance of the vote. *The Spectator* once put the point with great brevity and force when it wrote, "We dwell so strongly on the franchise because it includes all other rights, and is the one essential thing." Now this is either true or untrue; if true it applies to women as well as to "Uitlanders." After thinking of the war and its causes the first thing in the morning and the last thing at night for nearly three years, there were many thousands of Englishwomen who asked themselves why, if the vote to Englishmen in the Transvaal was worth £200,000,000 of money and some

30,000 lives, it was not also of great value and significance to women at home. Why, they said to themselves and to others, are we to be treated as perpetual "Uitlanders" in the country of our birth, which we love as well as any other of its citizens?

Therefore in the long run the war, though it temporarily caused a suspension of the suffrage agitation, nourished it at its source, and very shortly after the declaration of peace it became more active than it had ever been before. Ever since 1897, when Mr. Faithfull Begg's Women's Suffrage Bill had been read a second time by 228 to 157, the enemies of suffrage in the House of Commons had managed to evade a vote on a direct issue. The days obtained for Suffrage Bills were absorbed by the Government or merged into the holidays. One or other of the hundred ways of burking discussion open to the experienced Parliamentarian was used. Nevertheless women's suffrage resolutions were brought forward in 1904 and 1905; that of 1905 was "talked out."

At the end of 1905 the general public first became aware of a new element in the suffrage movement. The Women's Social and Political Union had been formed by Mrs. and Miss Pankhurst in 1903, but the "militant movement," with which its name will always be associated, had not attracted any public notice till the end of 1905. Its manifestations and multifarious activities have been set forth in detail by Miss Sylvia Pankhurst in a book, and are also so well known from other sources that it is unnecessary to dwell upon them here.[30] It is enough to say that by adopting novel and startling methods not at the outset associated with physical violence or attempts at violence, they succeeded in drawing a far larger amount of public attention to the claims of women to representation than ever had been given to the subject before. These methods were regarded by many suffragists with strong aversion, while others watched them with sympathy and admiration for the courage and self-sacrifice which these new methods involved. It is notorious that differences of method separate people from one another even more acutely than differences of aim. This has been seen in the history of religion as well as in politics: — "Christians have burnt each other, quite persuaded/ That the apostles would have done as they did."

It was a most anxious time for many months when there seemed a danger that the suffrage cause might degenerate into futile quarrelling among suffragists about the respective merits of their different methods, rather than develop into a larger, broader, and more widespread movement. This danger has been happily averted, partly by the good sense of the suffragists of all parties, who held firmly to the sheet anchor of the fact that they were all working for precisely the same thing, the removal of the sex disability in Parliamentary elections, and, therefore,

---

[30] See *The Suffragette*, by Miss E. Sylvia Pankhurst (Gay and Hancock, 1911).

that what united them was more important than that which separated them. The formation of the anti-suffrage societies was also from this point of view most opportune, giving us all an immediate objective. It was obvious to all suffragists that they should turn their artillery on their opponents rather than on each other. Therefore, while recognising fully all the acute differences which must exist between the advocates of revolutionary and constitutional methods, each group went on its own way; and the total result has undoubtedly been an extraordinary growth in the vigour and force of the suffrage movement all over the country. The most satisfactory feature of the situation was that however acute were the differences between the heads of the different societies, the general mass of suffragists throughout the country were loyal to the cause by whomsoever it was represented, just as Italian patriots in the great days of the *Risorgimento* supported the unity of Italy, whether promoted by Cavour, Garibaldi, or Mazzini.[31]

The National Union of Women's Suffrage Societies endeavoured to steer an even keel. They never weakened in their conviction that constitutional agitation was not only right in itself, but would prove far more effective in the long run than any display of physical violence, as a means of converting the electorate, the general public, and, consequently, Parliament and the Government, to a belief

---

[31] See *Garibaldi and the Making of Italy*, by G. M. Trevelyan, p. 3.

in women's suffrage. But the difficulties for a long time were very great. A few of our own members attacked us because we were not militant; others resigned because they disapproved of the militantism which we had repudiated. On one such occasion a high dignitary of the Church of England, who is also a distinguished historian, wrote to resign his position as vice-president of one of our societies because he highly disapproved of the recent action of the members of militant societies. The honorary secretary replied, asking him if he was also relinquishing his connection with Christianity, as she gathered from his writings that he strongly disapproved of what some Christians had done in the supposed interests of Christianity. It is to the credit of both that the threatened resignation was withdrawn. We tried to comfort and help the weak-hearted by reminding them, in the words of Viscount Morley, that "No reformer is fit for his task if he suffers himself to be frightened by the excesses of an extreme wing."[32]

Personally it was to myself the most difficult time of my forty years of suffrage work. I was helped a good deal by recalling a saying of my husband's about the Irish situation in the 'eighties, when he was heard saying to himself, "Just keep on and do what is right." I am far from claiming that we actually accomplished the difficult feat of doing what was right, but I believe we tried to. But the brutal

---

[32] Morley's *Life of Gladstone*, vol. iii. p. 371.

severity with which some of the militant suffragists were treated gave suffragists of all parties another subject on which they were in agreement.

Minor breaches of the law, such as waving flags and making speeches in the lobbies of the Houses of Parliament, were treated more severely than serious crime on the part of men has often been. A sentence of three months' imprisonment as an ordinary offender was passed in one case against a young girl who had done nothing except to decline to be bound over to keep the peace which she was prepared to swear she had not broken. The turning of the hose upon a suffrage prisoner in her cell in a midwinter night, and all the anguish of the hunger strike and forcible feeding are other examples. All through 1908 and 1909 a dead set was made upon law-breakers, real or supposed, who were obscure and unknown; while people with well-known names and of good social position were treated with leniency, and in some cases were allowed to do almost anything without arrest or punishment.[33]

The militant societies split into two in 1907, when the Freedom League was formed under the Presidency of Mrs. Despard. Shortly after this both the militant groups abandoned the plan upon which for the first few years they had worked — that of suffering violence, but using none. Stone-throwing of a not very formidable kind was

---

[33] I have in my possession positive proof that orders were given to the police not to arrest a particular lady whose name is well known and highly respected in every part of the country.

indulged in, and personal attacks upon Ministers of the Crown were attempted.[34] These new developments necessitated, in the opinion of the National Union of Women's Suffrage Societies, the publication of protests expressing their grave and strong objection to the use of personal violence as a means of political propaganda. These protests were published in November 1908 and October 1909.[35] The second, and shortest, was as follows:

—

"That the Council of the National Union of Women's Suffrage Societies strongly condemns the use of violence in political propaganda, and being convinced that the true way of advocating the cause of Women's Suffrage is by energetic, law-abiding propaganda, reaffirms its adherence to constitutional principles, and instructs the Executive Committee and the Societies to communicate this resolution to the Press."

To this was added: —

"That while condemning methods of violence the Council of the N.U.W.S.S. also protests most earnestly against the manner in which the whole Suffrage agitation has been handled by the responsible Government."

The National Union has not thought it necessary publicly to protest against every individual act of violence. Having

---

[34] I am requested by the Women's Freedom League to state that they have never resorted to stone-throwing or to personal assaults.

[35] A third protest was published in December 1911.

definitely and in a full Council, where all the societies in the Union are represented in proportion to their membership, put upon record that they "strongly condemn the use of violence in political propaganda," it appears unnecessary to asseverate that they condemn individual acts of violence. There is a remarkable passage in one of Cromwell's letters explaining why that which is gained by force is of little value in comparison with that which is conceded to the claims of justice and reason. "Things obtained by force," he wrote, "though never so good in themselves, would be both less to their honour and less likely to last than concessions made to argument and reason." "What we gain in a free way is better than twice as much in a forced, and will be more truly ours and our posterity's."[36] The practical example of male revolutionists is often cited to the contrary; but with all due respect to the other sex, is not their example too often an example of how not to do it? The Russian revolution, for instance, seems to have thrown the political development of Russia into a vicious circle: "we murder you because you and your like have murdered us," and thus it goes on in an endless vista like one mirror reflecting another. I admit fully that the kind and degree of violence carried out by the so-called "suffragettes" is of the mildest description; a few panes of glass have been broken, and meetings have been disturbed, but no one has suffered in life or limb; our

---

[36] Morley's *Life of Oliver Cromwell*, pp. 232-3.

great movement towards freedom has not been stained by serious crime. Compared with the Irish Nationalist movement in the 'eighties, or the recent unrest in India, the so-called "violence" of the suffragettes is absolutely negligible in degree, except as an indication of their frame of mind.

Far more violence has been suffered by the suffragettes than they have caused their opponents to suffer. The violence of the stewards at Liberal meetings in throwing out either men or women who dared to ask questions about women's suffrage has been most discreditable. It may be hoped it has been checked by an action claiming damages brought on at the Leeds Assizes in March 1911 on behalf of a man who had had his leg broken by the violence with which he had been thrown out of a meeting at Bradford by Liberal stewards, in the previous November. The judge ruled that his ejection from the meeting was in itself unlawful, and the only question he left to the jury was to assess damages. The jury awarded the plaintiff £100; this decision was appealed against, but the appeal was withdrawn in October 1911.[37]

Mark Twain once wrote of the women suffragists in his own country, "For forty years they have swept an imposingly large number of unfair laws from the statute books of America. In this brief time these serfs have set

---

[37] See Summing up of Mr. Justice Avory in Hawkins v. Muff case. *A Warning to Liberal Stewards*, published by the Men's Political Union, 1911.

themselves free — essentially. *Men could not have done as much for themselves in that time without bloodshed*, at least they never have, and that is an argument that they didn't know how."[38]

Perhaps the mild degree of violence perpetrated by the suffragettes was intended to lower our sex pride; we were going to show the world how to gain reforms without violence, without killing people and blowing up buildings, and doing the other silly things that men have done when they wanted the laws altered. Lord Acton once wrote: "It seems to be a law of political evolution that no great advance in human freedom can be gained except after the display of some kind of violence." We wanted to show that we could make the grand advance in human freedom, at which we aimed without the display of any kind of violence. We have been disappointed in that ambition, but we may still lay the flattering unction to our souls that the violence offered has not been formidable, and that the fiercest of the suffragettes have been far more ready to suffer pain than to inflict it. What those endured who underwent the hunger strike and the anguish of forcible feeding can hardly be overestimated. Their courage made a very deep impression on the public and touched the imagination of the whole country.

Of course a very different measure is applied to men and women in these matters, Women are expected to be able to

---

[38] *More Tramps Abroad*, by Mark Twain, p. 208.

bear every kind of injustice without even "a choleric word"; if men riot when they do not get what they want they are leniently judged, and excesses of which they may be guilty are excused in the House of Commons, in the press, and on the bench on the plea of political excitement. Compare the line of the press on the strike riots in Wales and elsewhere with the tone of the same papers on the comparatively infinitesimal degree of violence shown by the militant suffragists. No one has been more severe in his condemnation of militantism than Mr. Churchill, but speaking in the House of Commons in August 8, 1911, about the violent riots in connection with Parliamentary Reform in 1832, he is reported to have said: "It is true there was rioting in 1832, *but the people had no votes then, and had very little choice as to the alternatives they should adopt.*" If this is a good argument, why not extend its application to the militant suffragists?

The use of physical violence by the militant societies was not the only difference between them and the National Union. The two groups between 1905 and 1911 adopted different election policies. The militants believed, and they had much ground for their belief, that the only chance of a Women's Suffrage Bill being carried into law lay in its adoption by one or other of the great political parties as a party question. The private member, they urged, had no longer a chance of passing an important measure; it must be backed by a Government. Hence they concluded that the individual member of Parliament was of no particular consequence, and they concentrated their efforts at each electoral contest in endeavouring to coerce the Government of the day to take up the suffrage cause. Their cry in every election was "Keep the Liberal out," not, as they asserted, from party motives, but because the Government of the day, and the Government alone, had the power to pass a Suffrage Bill; and as long as any Government declined to take up suffrage they would have to encounter all the opposition which the militants could command. In carrying out this policy they opposed the strongest supporters of women's suffrage if they were also supporters of the Government.

The National Union adopted a different election policy — that of obtaining declarations of opinion from all candidates at each election and supporting the man, independent of party, who gave the most satisfactory assurances of support. In the view of the National Union this policy was infinitely more adapted to the facts of the situation than that adopted by the militants. What was desired was that the electorate should be educated in the principles of women's suffrage, and made to understand what women wanted, and why they wanted it; and electors were much more likely to approach the subject in a reasonable frame of mind if they had not been thrown into a violent rage by what they considered an unfair attack upon their own party. To this it was replied that only the Liberals were enraged and that the Conservatives would be correspondingly conciliated. It did not appear, however, that this was actually the case. The Conservatives were not slow to see that their immunity from attack was only temporary; when their turn came to have a Government in power the cry would be changed to "Keep the Conservative out." And then having profoundly irritated one half of the electorate, the militants would go on to irritate the other half. What the National Union aimed at was the creation in each constituency of a Women's Suffrage society on non-party lines, which should by meetings, articles, and educational propaganda of all kinds create so strong a feeling in favour of women's suffrage as to make party managers on both sides realise, in choosing candidates, that they would have a better chance of success with a man who was a suffragist than with a man who was an anti-suffragist.

The whole Parliamentary situation was altered when in November 1910, and again more explicitly in June and August 1911, Mr. Asquith promised on behalf of the Government that on certain conditions they would grant time for all the stages of a Women's Suffrage Bill during this Parliament. This removed the basis on which the militant societies had founded their election policy; it no longer was an impossibility for a private member to carry a Reform Bill, and it became obvious that the road to success lay in endeavouring, as far as possible, to promote the return of men of all parties to the House of Commons who were genuine suffragists. The Women's Social and Political Union and the Freedom League appreciated the importance of this change, and early in 1911 they definitely suspended militant action, and abandoned their original election policy. There was thus harmony in methods as well as unity of aims between the Suffrage Societies until this harmony was disturbed by the events to be described in the next chapter.

CHAPTER VII
RECENT DEVELOPMENTS

"If a great change is to be made in human affairs, the minds of men will be fitted to it; the general opinions and feelings will draw that way. Every fear, every hope will forward it, and then they who persist in opposing this mighty current in human affairs, will appear rather to resist the decrees of Providence itself, than the mere designs of men. They will not be resolute and firm, but perverse and obstinate." — Burke (*Thoughts on French Affairs*).

The Parliament elected in January 1906 contained an overwhelming Liberal majority; it also contained more than 400 members, belonging to all parties, who were pledged to the principle of women's suffrage. A considerable number of these had expressed their adherence to the movement in their election addresses.

Mr. (now Viscount) Haldane had said at Reading, just before the election, that he considered women's suffrage not only desirable, but necessary, if Parliament would grapple successfully with the difficult problems of social reform. Mr. Lloyd George stigmatised the exclusion of women from the right of voting as "an act of intolerable injustice." Sir Henry Campbell Bannerman, the Prime Minister, who received a deputation containing representatives of all the suffrage societies in May 1906, said that they "had made out a conclusive and irrefutable case." Still no promise of Government help for the passing of a Suffrage Bill was forthcoming; the difference of opinion in both parties on the subject of women's suffrage cut across all party ties, and thus hindered Government action. It was obvious that no private member, in the changed conditions of modern politics, could pass so important a Bill without Government help; and no promise of this help could be obtained. The first debate on a Women's Suffrage Bill in the new Parliament took place in 1907, when the speaker refused to grant the closure and the Bill was talked out. Mr. Stanger, K.C., M.P., drew a good place in the ballot in 1908, and his Bill for the simple removal of the sex disability from existing franchises came on for second reading in February. The closure having been granted, the division resulted in the great majority for the Bill of 273 to 94. But no further progress was made.

In May of the same year a deputation of Liberal M.P.'s waited on Mr. Asquith, who had then become Prime Minister, to press him for aid for passing into law a Women's Suffrage Bill. He admitted that about two-thirds of his Cabinet and a majority of his party were favourable to women's suffrage, and while maintaining his own continued opposition to it, made a statement that his Government intended to introduce a measure of electoral reform, and that if an amendment for the admission of women were proposed on democratic lines, his Government as a Government would not oppose it. This was a great advance on the position occupied by Mr. Gladstone in 1884, when he vehemently opposed a women's suffrage amendment to the Reform Bill of that year. All the organs of public opinion without exception recognised that this promise advanced the movement for women's suffrage to a higher place in practical politics than it had ever before occupied. The next year, 1909, Mr. Geoffrey Howard, M.P., and other Liberal members abandoned the non-party Women's Suffrage Bill which had hitherto always been introduced, and brought forward a Bill for what was practically universal adult suffrage; this course alienated all Conservative and much moderate Liberal support, and was taken in the face of the strongly expressed protests of all the suffrage societies. The division on the second reading showed a majority of only 35 or less than one-fifth of the majority for the more moderate Bill. The supporters fell in numbers from 273 to 159, and the opposition increased from 94 to 124, and this in a House of Commons with the immense combined Liberal, Labour, and Nationalist majority of 513 to 157. In the House of Commons elected successively in January and December 1910 the same combination of parties had a majority of about 125, as compared with a majority of 356 in the Parliament of 1906. These figures are most eloquent of the real political situation, and explain why genuine suffragists who want women's names on the register before the next election, supported, in the absence of Government aid, a measure on moderate lines calculated to unite the greatest amount of support from all parts of the House, rather than a Bill drafted on extreme party lines, which would certainly alienate Conservative and moderate Liberal support. If an Adult Suffrage Bill could only obtain a majority of 35 when the Government majority was 356, it is easy to predict where it would be when the Government majority was reduced to 125.

In December 1909 the Government announced an immediate dissolution of Parliament. For the first time in the history of the women's suffrage movement the political campaign preceding a general election was opened with important declarations from the Prime Minister and other members of his Government on the subject of the enfranchisement of women.

At the great meeting of his party at the Albert Hall, December 10, 1909, after indicating his own continued opposition to women's suffrage, Mr. Asquith said: "Nearly two years ago I declared on behalf of the present Government that in the event, which we then contemplated, of our bringing in a Reform Bill, we should make the insertion of a suffrage amendment an open question for the House of Commons to decide (cheers). Our friends and fellow workers of the Women's Liberal Federation (cheers) have asked me to say that my declaration survives the expiring Parliament, and will hold good in its successor, and that their cause, so far as the Government is concerned, shall be no worse off in the new Parliament than it would have been in the old. I have no hesitation in acceding to that request (cheers). The Government ... has no disposition or desire to burke this question; it is clearly an issue on which the new House of Commons ought to be given an opportunity to express its views."

On the same day Sir Edward Grey, at Alnwick, reiterated his continued support of women's suffrage. In reply to a question, he said: "If that means, am I in favour of a reasonable Bill for giving votes to women, I have always supported that Bill, and I don't think it right to change my opinions because what I believe to be a small minority among women has been very violent and unreasonable." Mr. Winston Churchill, a few days earlier, expressed a similar opinion to that of Sir Edward Grey.

The anti-suffragists are never weary of asserting that women's suffrage has never been before the country as a practical political issue. It is difficult to imagine what being "before the country" consists in, if the foregoing declarations on the part of the leaders of the party in power do not indicate that a question has reached this stage. At the general election of January 1910, 245 candidates mentioned in their election addresses that they supported the extension of the Parliamentary franchise to women.[39]

---

[39] See the Annual Report of the National Union of Women's Suffrage Societies presented in March 1910.

In this election the National Union organised a voters' petition in support of women's suffrage. The signatures, amounting to over 280,000, were nearly all collected on polling day from electors who had just recorded their own vote. In some constituencies, especially in the North of England, hardly a man refused his signature; the polling number was in each case attached to the signature as a means of identification, and as a guarantee of good faith. No objection has ever been made to our petitions, or signatures disallowed, as in the case of some of the anti-suffrage petitions, on the ground that there were pages of signatures all in the same handwriting.

An extremely important event in the development of the suffrage movement in the field of practical politics took place almost simultaneously with the January 1910 election. This was the formation of the Conciliation Committee. It was recognised on all hands that women's suffrage was in an unprecedented Parliamentary position; a large majority of members of Parliament were pledged to it, but it was not backed by either of the great parties, and consequently lacked the driving power to get through the stages necessary to convert a Bill into an Act of Parliament. This was in part due to differences as to the sort of women's suffrage which members of Parliament were prepared to accept. The Liberals objected to a Bill in the old lines based on the removal of the sex disability, dreading that such a measure would be used as a means of multiplying plural voting, and would thus probably tell heavily against the Liberal party. Conservatives and moderate Liberals objected to the immense addition to the electorate which would be caused by adult suffrage. The Conciliation Committee was formed with the view of reconciling these differences, by finding a Bill which all suffragists could support. With the exception of the chairman, the Earl of Lytton, and the Hon. Secretary, Mr. H. N. Brailsford, it consisted entirely of members of the House of Commons favourable to women's suffrage, and representing the parties — Liberal, Conservative, Labour, and Nationalist — into which the House is divided. As the result of the work of this committee a Bill was arrived at, to which all the parties represented on the committee could agree.

The Bill was drafted on the lines of simple Household Suffrage with a clause expressly laying down that marriage was not to be a disqualification. It has never been contended that this is a perfect Bill; it was the result of a compromise between the different parties in the House of Commons. The Conservatives and moderate Liberals objected to adult suffrage; the Liberals and their allies objected to the old suffrages being simply opened to women for the reasons just indicated; therefore, in deference to Liberal objections, the freeholders, occupiers, service, university, lodger, and other franchises were abandoned in the case of women, and in deference to Conservative objections adult suffrage was not proposed. The Bill which was agreed upon was based upon the democratic principle of Household Suffrage, of which the country had had more than forty years' experience as far as women were concerned in municipal elections. The principle of the Conciliation Bill is to make Household Suffrage a reality. Mrs. Humphry Ward condemns this measure as "absurd."[40] Wherein its absurdity consists she does not explain. Household Suffrage was the main sheet anchor of all the great Reform Bills of the last century; it is the basis of most of the local franchises. It is by far the most important, numerically, of all the various existing franchises. An interesting return is published every year of the total number of Parliamentary voters, indicating the qualifications under which they vote. That dated February 28, 1911, shows that in the whole United Kingdom there were 7,705,602 registered electors; of these 6,716,742 voted as occupiers and householders, while less than 1,000,000 represented the total of all the other franchises put together. The Bill, therefore, which gives women Household Suffrage admits them to by far the most important suffrage which men enjoy. Personally many suffragists would prefer a less restricted measure, but the immense importance and gain to our movement in getting the most effective of all the existing franchises thrown open to women cannot be exaggerated. This was immediately appreciated by all the suffrage societies and also by the Women's Liberal Federation, all of which gave

---

[40] *Standard*, Oct. 17, 1911.

hearty and enthusiastic support to the Bill, known as the Conciliation Bill, to extend Household Suffrage to women.[41]

The Conciliation Committee and the suffrage societies successfully refuted the charge made against the Conciliation Bill that it was undemocratic. It would, if passed, enfranchise approximately 1,000,000 women, and it was proved conclusively, by careful analysis of the social status of women householders in a large and representative group of constituencies, that the overwhelming majority of these would be working-class women. In London (1908) the proportion of working-class women was shown to be 87 per cent., in Dundee (1910), 89 per cent., Bangor and Carnarvon (1910), 75 per cent. The average in about fifty representative constituencies, where the investigation was conducted under the auspices of the Independent Labour Party, was shown to be 82 per cent. The Bill gave no representation to property whatever. The only qualification which it recognised was that of the resident householder.

This Bill, drawn in such a way as not to admit of amendment, was introduced by Mr. Shackleton, Labour

---

[41] See resolution adopted by the executive committee of the Women's Liberal Federation, quoted in *Standard*, October 30, 1911:- "That ... the executive resolves that until definite promises are made of a Government Reform Bill including women they will support by all means in their power the Bill promoted by the Conciliation Committee and will pursue with regard to amendments to that Bill such a policy as circumstances show to be most likely to secure for it a substantial third reading majority."

member for Clitheroe in the new Parliament, elected in January 1910. Two days of Government time were given for its second reading in July of that year. It was the first time a Women's Suffrage Bill had been the subject of a full-dress debate. Parliamentary leaders on both sides took part in it, and the voting was left to the free judgment of the House of Commons. Among the supporters of the Bill were Mr. (now Viscount) Haldane, Mr. Arthur Balfour, Mr. Philip Snowden, and Mr. W. Redmond, while among its opponents were Mr. Asquith, Mr. Austen Chamberlain, Mr. F. E. Smith, and Mr. Haviland Burke. Mr. Lloyd George and Mr. Winston Churchill also vehemently opposed the Bill, not on the ground of opposition to women's enfranchisement, but because of the alleged undemocratic character of this particular measure, and because it was introduced in a form that did not admit of amendment. The division resulted in the large majority of 110 for the second reading, a figure in excess of anything which the Government could command for their chief party measures.

Notwithstanding this large majority the Bill was destined to make no further progress that session; but the interval between the second reading and the assembling of Parliament for the autumn session was utilised for the organisation of the most remarkable series of public demonstrations of an entirely peaceful character which have probably ever been held in this country in support of any extension of the suffrage. It was estimated that no fewer than 4000 public meetings were held in the four months between July and November; the largest halls all over the country were filled again and again; the Albert Hall was filled twice in one week; the largest meeting ever held in Hyde Park, when more than half a million of people were assembled, was organised by the Women's Social and Political Union. It was at this moment that the remarkable movement, already referred to in Chapter V., was begun — the series of petitions from Town and other locally elected Councils for the speedy passing into law of the measure known as the Conciliation Bill. The city of Glasgow led the way with a unanimous vote of its Council.

During this autumn Sir Edward Grey, Mr. Birrell, and Mr. Runciman made public declarations in support of women's suffrage, and said that in their opinion facilities for the further progress of the Bill and its passage into law ought to be provided in 1911. A few months later Lord Haldane said he hoped "the Bill would pass quickly." The most important practical gain for the suffrage movement was, however, achieved in November 1910. Early in the month Mr. Asquith had announced the intention of his Government again immediately to dissolve Parliament; and on the 22nd, in reply to a question in the House, he said that the Government would, "if they were still in power, give facilities in the next Parliament for effectively proceeding with a [Women's Suffrage] Bill, if so framed as to admit of free amendment." These words gave to suffragists the key which enabled them to unlock the doors which barred their progress. The more astute political minds among the anti-suffragists immediately saw the importance of this promise. *The Times,* November 24, announced that it made women's suffrage an issue before the country at the coming election, and added, "If the election confirms the Government in power the new Parliament *will be considered to have received a mandate on the subject of women's suffrage.*"[42]

The feather-heads could see nothing of any importance in this promise, and the *Anti-Suffrage Review* allowed itself the treat of entitling an article "Nod and wink promises." All suffragists of any experience, however, felt that their cause had received an immensely important impetus, and that they were gaining ground not by painful inches but by furlongs. When the session of 1911 opened, the Conciliation Committee was again formed, and good luck smiled upon its members, for three of them drew the first, second, and third places in the ballot, and thus secured an excellent place for the second reading of the Bill. The member in charge was Sir George Kemp, who sits for N.W. Manchester. The Bill was, of course, drawn so as to admit of free amendment. The second reading was on May 5, 1911, and there voted for it 255, and against it 88. The majority of 110 in 1910 had thus grown in 1911 to 167. There were 55 pairs; but the number of members wishing to pair in favour of the Bill was so great that the

---

[42] See "Political Notes," *Times,* November 24, 1910.

demand could not be satisfied. Six of these wrote to the papers explaining their position.

Almost immediately after this an announcement was made from the front bench that Mr. Asquith's promise of the previous November that an opportunity should be given for proceeding with the Bill in all its stages would be fulfilled during the session of 1912. There was for a time some fencing and difficulty over the point whether this promise applied exclusively to the Conciliation Bill or to any Women's Suffrage Bill which might obtain a place in the ballot for second reading. All doubt on this subject was finally set at rest on August 23, by a letter from Mr. Asquith to Lord Lytton, in which the Prime Minister stated that the promises were given in regard to the Conciliation Bill, and that they would be strictly adhered to both in letter and in spirit.

This, then, was the position of the suffrage question between the close of the summer session and the beginning of November 1911. All the suffrage societies were working in complete harmony on the same lines and for the same Bill. The militant societies had suspended militant tactics, and also their anti-government election policy. The Women's Liberal Federation, whose co-operation was of great and obvious importance, were uniting their efforts with those of the suffrage societies, when on November 7, a bombshell was dropped among them in the speech of the Prime Minister, replying to a deputation from the People's Suffrage Federation, who presented a memorial asking for adult suffrage. Mr. Asquith then announced that it was the intention of his Government to introduce during the coming session (1912) the Electoral Reform Bill, which he had foreshadowed in 1908, that all existing franchises would be swept away, plural voting abolished, and the period of residence reduced. The new franchise was to be based on citizenship, and votes were to be given "to citizens of full age and competent understanding." But no place was found within the four comers of the Bill for the enfranchisement of women. Mr. Asquith reiterated his promise of facilities for the Conciliation Bill, and then merely dismissed the subject of women's suffrage with the remark that his opinions upon it were well known. If it had been his object to enrage every women's suffragist to the point of frenzy, he could not have acted with greater perspicacity. Years of unexampled effort and self-sacrifice had been expended by women to force upon the Government the enfranchisement of women, and when the Prime Minister spoke the only promise he made was to give more votes to men. Mrs. Bernard Shaw exactly expressed the sentiments of women's suffragists, whether militant or non-militant, when she wrote that Mr. Asquith's speech filled her with "an impulse of blind rage"; she felt she had been personally insulted, and that he had said to her in effect "that the vilest male wretch who can contrive to keep a house of ill-fame shall have a vote, and that the noblest woman in England shall not have one because she is a female" (*The Times*, November 21, 1911).

It is never safe to act under an impulse of blind rage, and very soon a closer knowledge of the actual facts surrounding and explaining the situation brought the conviction home to many of us, indeed it may be stated to the whole body of suffragists with one important exception,[43] that the new situation created by Mr. Asquith's speech, so far from decreasing the chances of success for women's suffrage in 1912 had very greatly strengthened them. First of all we were cheered by the courageous and outspoken remonstrances on behalf of women made by *The Manchester Guardian* and *The Nation. The Manchester Guardian*, (November 9, 1911), said that the exclusion of women would be "an outrage and, we hope, an impossibility.... No Government calling itself Liberal could so far betray Liberal principles without incurring deep and lasting discredit and ultimate disaster." The Labour party, through its chairman, Mr. Ramsay MacDonald, M.P., also spoke out very plainly. "We shall take care," he said, "that the Manhood Suffrage Bill is not used to destroy the success of the women's agitation, *because we have to admit that it has been the women's agitation that has brought the question of the franchise both for men and women to the front at the present time.*"

---

[43] The Woman's Social and Political Union dissented from this view. They resumed militant tactics, and scenes of considerable disorder occurred on November 21 and November 29, 1911.

Like other experienced Parliamentarians, he advised us to hold the Government to their pledges about the Conciliation Bill until we had actually secured something better (*The Manchester Guardian*, November 9, 1911).

Then we began to hear from those we knew we could trust of meetings that were being held of suffrage members of the Government to decide upon a plan of action, so as to secure for women a better chance of enfranchisement through the operation of an amendment to the Government Bill than we could have if we relied upon the Conciliation Bill alone. An invitation was received from the Prime Minister to all the suffrage societies to attend a deputation on the subject. The full report of that deputation was in all the papers of November 18, 1911. It is sufficient here to say that when Mr. Asquith spoke he acknowledged the strength and intensity of the demand for women's suffrage, and admitted that in opposing it he was in a minority both in his Cabinet and in his party; finally, and most important of all, he added that although he could not initiate and propose the change which women were seeking, he was prepared to bow to, and acquiesce in, the deliberate judgment of the House of Commons, and that it was quite in accordance with the best traditions of English public life that he should act thus. A great majority of those who were present thought that the Prime Minister had recognised that women's suffrage was inevitable, and that it would not be for the benefit of his party that he should withstand to the last this great advance in human freedom.

Mr. Asquith gave positive and definite answers in the affirmative to the four questions which were asked by the National Union of Women's Suffrage Societies: —

1. Is it the intention of the Government that the Reform Bill shall go through all its stages in 1912?

2. Will the Bill be drafted in such a way as to admit of any amendments introducing women on other terms than men?

3. Will the Government undertake not to oppose such amendments?

4. Will the Government regard any amendment enfranchising woman which is carried as an integral part of the Bill in all its stages?[44]

Almost immediately after this Mr. Lloyd George authorised the public announcement that he was himself prepared to move the women's suffrage amendment to the Reform Bill, or, if it was thought best in the interests of women's suffrage, he would be pleased to stand aside in favour of Sir Edward Grey or of some leading Conservative. It has been indicated very plainly that the amendment Mr. Lloyd George himself favours will be one for the enfranchisement of householders and wives of householders. A Bill to this effect has been some time before Parliament, and is familiarly known as Dickinson, No. 2; it enacts that when a husband and wife reside

---

[44] These speeches can be obtained from the Women's Liberal Federation, 2 Victoria Street, London, S.W.

together in premises for which, under the existing law, the husband is entitled to vote, the wife shall also be entitled to vote as a joint-occupier. There is a parallel for a provision of this kind in the existing franchise law of Norway. Sir Edward Grey, Mr. Lloyd George, Mr. Ramsay MacDonald, and other suffragists in and out of the House of Commons concur in the opinion that the present situation gives our movement almost a certainty of success in the session of 1912.

Mr. Lloyd George opened his campaign for women's suffrage in an important speech at Bath on November 24, 1911. It was a men's meeting, the occasion being the Annual Congress of the Liberal Federation. He was received with enthusiasm and made a powerful and well-reasoned speech in favour of the enfranchisement of women. This was followed in December 16 by a meeting in London of the Women's Liberal Federation addressed by Sir Edward Grey and Mr. Lloyd George.[45] The former dwelt upon the reasons which weighed with him in favour of the representation of women, and indicated that the amendment to the Reform Bill which he favoured would be on the lines of Women's Suffrage in Norway, i.e. not Adult Suffrage, but suffrage for women householders, including wives (as indicated on p. 81). Mr. Lloyd George dwelt on the essential partnership of men and women in all

---

[45] The Corporation of Dublin authorised the Lord Mayor and other officers to attend in their robes and present the Dublin petition in person at the Bar of the House of Commons.

the greatest things in human life, and urged that this partnership should be extended to politics. Thus the year 1911 ended with every prospect of a hard won Parliamentary victory for women's suffrage in 1912. Women's suffrage always has been, and will remain, a non-party question. The Conservative and Unionist Women's Franchise Association is working as keenly as any of the other suffrage societies. We shall not succeed in 1912 unless we are successful in attracting the support of Conservatives as well as Liberals and Radicals. To aid us in the final struggle it is of no little value that we have the promise of a week's Government time for the Conciliation Bill, if our hopes of carrying a satisfactory amendment to the Reform Bill should be frustrated.

We are on the eve of the fulfilment of our hopes. The goal towards which many of us have been striving for nearly half a century is in sight. I appeal to each and all of my fellow-suffragists not to be over confident, but so to act as if the success of the suffrage cause depended on herself alone. And even if our anticipated victory should be once more delayed, I appeal to them again not to despond but to stand firm and fast, and be prepared to work on as zealously and as steadfastly as of old.

A splendid lesson reaches us from America. The great victory for women's suffrage in California in October 1911 was at first reported to be a defeat. A group of the leaders, including Dr. Anna Shaw, had been sitting up to the small hours of the morning in the New York Women's

Suffrage Office, receiving news from California, 3000 miles away. The first returns were so bad that it looked as if nothing could save the situation; and the grief was all the greater because victory had been confidently counted on. Dr. Anna Shaw went away in deep despondency. Presently she came back saying she could not sleep, and walking backwards and forwards in the office, she explained a new plan of campaign which her fertile brain had already originated. This is the spirit which is unconquerable and it is our spirit too.

He who runs may read the signs of the times. Everything points to the growing volume and force of the women's movement. Even if victory should be delayed it cannot be delayed long. The suffragists ought to be the happiest of mankind, if happiness has been correctly defined as the perpetual striving for an object of supreme excellence and constantly making a nearer approach to it.

Printed in Great Britain
by Amazon

86528554R00068